BIRDS
of the
CENTRAL ROCKIES

Jan Wassink

Mountain Press Publishing Company
Missoula, Montana
1991

Fourth Printing
April, 1997

Library of Congress Cataloging-in-Publication Data

Wassink, Jan L.
    Birds of the central Rockies / Jan Wassink.
        p.   cm.
    Includes index.
    ISBN 0-87842-235-8 : $14.00
    1. Birds—Rocky Mountains—Identification.   2. Birds—Rocky
Mountains—Pictorial works.   I. Title.
QL683.R63W37   1991   91-18652
598.2978—dc20   CIP

Printed in Hong by Mantec Production Company

Mountain Press Publishing Company
P.O. Box 2399, Missoula, MT 59806
(406) 728-1900

Dedicated to my sons,
Kip, Chad and Troy,
who have enriched my life
more than they will ever know.

Table of Contents

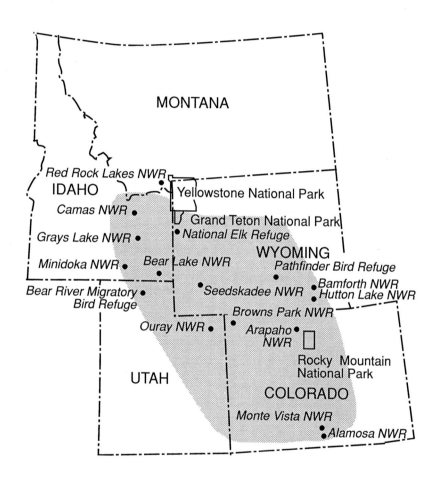

Map showing the central Rockies (shaded) and locations of national parks and wildlife refuges.

The Central Rockies

More than 180,000 square miles of mountainous terrain make up the central Rockies, extending from Yellowstone National Park in Wyoming to just north of the southern border of Colorado, from the prairies in the east to the desert country of the Great Basin in the west. The central Rockies are home to a rich and varied array of bird life. Birders seeking to glimpse this diversity can roam habitats from marshy shores, sagebrush flats and agricultural cropland in the valleys, to expansive montane forests at the mid-elevations and alpine meadows and mountaintops that exceed 14,000 feet. Fifteen national wildlife refuges—including Seedskadee National Wildlife Refuge in Wyoming, Browns Park and Alamosa national wildlife refuges in Colorado—protect important habitat for migrating and nesting waterfowl. Wilderness areas, national monuments, national recreation areas and national parks help to maintain the beauty and integrity of the region's wildlife habitats. The United States Forest Service and the Bureau of Land Management manage other wide expanses for multiple use, one of which is wildlife values. There can be little doubt that the central Rockies provide excellent opportunities for careful observers to enjoy the bounty of birdlife.

Great Gray Owl

J. L. Wassink

Introduction

I started watching birds more than twenty years ago. In the beginning, just seeing a brightly colored bird was excitement enough. But, very soon, I wasn't satisfied until I knew its name. I soon wondered, What does it eat? Where does it go in the winter? Where does it nest? Why do I only see it along riverbottoms?

Approximately thirty million other people in North America share my curiosity about birds, and more become interested every day. This book provides beginning birdwatchers with an easy-to-use field guide to some of the more common birds of the central Rockies. It also provides answers to many of the other questions you will ask as your interest in birds deepens and your knowledge expands.

How to Use this Book

The checklists of Rocky Mountain National Park, fifteen national wildlife refuges in Wyoming, Colorado, eastern Idaho and eastern Utah, as well as the "Colorado Bird Distribution Latilong Study" (see Suggested References) indicate that over 400 of North America's 800 or so species of birds have been observed in the central Rockies. Approximately 250 of those species live or visit here regularly and in sufficient numbers to be classified as "fairly common," "common" or "abundant." Most of the 191 species included in this book were selected from these 250 species based on ease of identification and the likelihood that a beginning birder will encounter it. The book also includes some less common species that illustrate the diversity of birdlife in the area, have interesting life histories or offer a striking appearance. At least one representative from each family of birds in the region is included.

With only a couple of exceptions to accommodate layout, the order of birds in this book follows the *Checklist of North American Birds*, sixth edition, published by the American Ornithologist's Union. For easy identification, a photo faces the description of each bird. To identify a bird, simply locate its photo in the book and glance across the page to learn its name. You will see two names there: a Latin name and a common name. The common name is probably the one you will learn first but the Latin name is also important because it will help you recognize relationships between different birds.

Scientists classify birds, like all living organisms, according to their physical similarities and differences. The seven divisions in this classification system are—from most general to most specific—kingdom, phylum, class, order, family, genus and species. The species includes individuals that exhibit virtually identical characteristics and breed with each other when given the opportunity. The genus consists of one or more species that are very similar to each other but do not interbreed. The names of the these two groups, the genus and the species, make up the Latin name. In this classification system each species has a unique scientific name. A scientist in Russia, reading about *Turdus migratorious*, knows that he is reading about the American robin and not the one found in Europe, which is a different species.

To avoid looking at every photo each time you wish to identify a new bird, study the general characteristics (size, shape, behavior and habitat) in the "family introductions," skim through the species descriptions and study the photos. When you can recognize an unfamiliar water bird as a grebe, you can go directly to the grebe photos for species identification without wasting time looking through the duck section as well.

If you spend much time birding, you will eventually see a bird that you cannot match with a photo in this book. In some species, the sexes are dimorphic (have different color patterns) and only the male is pictured here. You can often identify females of that species, particularly during the breeding season, by the company they keep. For example, if a male bufflehead is swimming alongside a small, brownish duck of approximately the same size and shape, check the written description of the female bufflehead. If that doesn't match, you may be viewing a species that is not included here. In other cases, there may be different color phases within the species. The snow goose, for instance, has a white and a "blue" phase, and many hawks exhibit more than one color phase. While both phases of the snow goose appear here, only the light phase of the ferruginous hawk, which also has a dark phase, is illustrated. For illustrations of species and color phases that this book does not cover, you will need to consult a more comprehensive field guide (see Suggested References).

The field marks section describes characteristics of the bird that you will probably be able to see in the field. The size, an important factor in identifying birds, leads the list. The measurements, in inches, indicate the length from the tip of the bill to the tip of the tail as seen in the wild. The measurements define an average length for that species; individuals may be larger or smaller. At first, you may have trouble differentiating between a five inch and a six inch bird, but, as you gain experience and develop a feel for the size of familiar species, you will begin to recognize that a new bird looks slightly larger or smaller than a familiar species. While many species may resemble each other superficially, each species has a unique combination of characteristics that distinguish it. Those identifying characteristics are highlighted with bold type. The rest of the field marks section outlines general features of the bird. The "Parts of a Bird" illustrations at the end of the book identify the terms used in this section.

The status relates the general areas of the region the bird occupies, the bird's abundance in those areas, the seasons to look for it there and the bird's breeding status in the region. I have abbreviated the names central Rockies (CR) and Rocky Mountain National Park (RMNP).

Definitions of abundance are subjective at best, but the following terms will prove helpful. An abundant bird is one that you are likely to see 25 or more of per day when looking in the appropriate habitat during the appropriate season. You will likely see a common bird daily when looking in the right habitat during the right season. Fairly common birds are likely to be seen once every three days and uncommon birds probably no more than once in a week of looking. Rare birds appear only a few times each year. Irregular species are abundant at times but extremely rare most of the time.

While the above terminology addresses only the numbers of a species that are present in the region, the following terminology describes when a bird might be seen here and whether it breeds while it is here. A resident bird lives in the region year-round, while a summer resident is present only in spring and summer. A breeder nests and raises young within the region. Winter visitors frequent the central Rockies between mid-December and the late February while migrants travel through the area on their annual spring and/or fall migrations. Vagrants do not normally visit the region but may occasionally wander through.

The main description of each bird deals with the bird's "niche"—how, when and where it feeds, builds its nest, attracts mates and whether its populations are increasing or decreasing. Look in the main description for distinctive behavior that can aid in identification. Be sure to check the family or subfamily descriptions for characteristics common to the whole group.

The calls or songs of most species are diagnostic once you know them. However, written descriptions of songs proved very little use to me when I started watching birds. I have only included written descriptions of songs and calls that are simple and very distinctive. When you reach the point where you want to learn to bird by sound, purchase one of the guides to bird songs in the Suggested References.

Observing Birds

There really is no "best place" to watch birds. Many people travel to national parks or wildlife refuges to view birds. And, if you are looking for a particular species that inhabits only one area or is particularly abundant there, that may be the best place to go. However, birding can easily fit into your daily activities. I do much of my birding while I am doing other things. I watch from my living room while I am relaxing or keeping one eye on a football game. I often bird in my backyard while feeding my llamas or doing yard work. I also do a lot of birding from my vehicle while on my way to or from work or other appointments.

When I devote time exclusively to birding, I do not really need to venture farther afield than my backyard—five acres of Douglas fir, a reclaimed apple orchard and numerous thickets and weed patches. Not only is it home to a wide variety of species but it is also readily accessible—I can sneak in a few minutes of birding before and after work or perhaps while I should be mowing the lawn! By finding a good place to bird close to home, you can familiarize yourself with that area and the birds that frequent it, where their territories are, where they feed, where they nest and how they behave.

Still, birding in new territory, looking for new species and watching huge concentrations of birds in staging areas or on breeding grounds is too exciting to overlook. To locate worthwhile sites, talk to local birders or check with your state wildlife officials and the wildlife refuges in the region. For example, the Colorado Division of Wildlife provides information and directions to several sagegrouse leks that are accessible for public viewing. One of the most spectacular sights in Colorado is the annual spring gathering of more than 17,000 sandhill cranes in the San Luis Valley in and around the Monte Vista and Alamosa National Wildlife Refuges.

Blue grouse begins its courting ritual.   J. L. Wassink

The best time to watch birds is anytime you can. But, you will greatly increase your viewing success and enjoyment if you look for certain birds when they are most active. For example, if you want to see owls, look for them at night (except for the few diurnal species). Likewise, if you wish to observe the small songbirds, look for them in the few hours just after dawn when they are the most vocal and active.

You can often bird very effectively from your vehicle by stopping and scanning suitable habitats with binoculars. But, it is often more enjoyable to get out, walk slowly and quietly through the area and use your ears as well as your eyes to locate birds. Once you hear a song or see a movement, concentrate on that spot until you can pinpoint the bird with your binoculars and identify it. Often, the birds will quiet down and stop moving around when you first walk into an area and you may think there is not a living creature within miles. Sit down or stand and wait quietly and you may soon be surrounded by birds as they resume their normal activities.

Attracting Birds

Birds live only where they can satisfy their basic requirements of food, water, cover and nesting sites. During winter, you can use bird feeders to provide the food portion of the equation and attract birds to your yard. Most grocery, variety and feed stores carry a selection of inexpensive feeders and stock sunflower seeds and mixed seeds. Place the feeder in the open near a tree or bush large enough to provide cover for the birds and in a spot easily visible from the house.

Offering sunflower seeds, mixed seeds, suet and peanut butter in feeders on our front deck, we enjoy birding while going about our daily activities. In summer, we also add sugar water feeders for the hummingbirds. As I write this, on a cold snowy afternoon, I am watching American goldfinches, mourning doves, downy woodpeckers, northern flickers, black-billed magpies, mountain chickadees, black-capped chickadees, red-breasted nuthatches and evening grosbeaks reduce my seed supply.

You can also provide food and attract birds by carefully choosing your landscaping. Plant fruit trees or berry bushes to attract fruit-loving birds or provide plants with nectar-bearing flowers to entice nectar-loving species such as hummingbirds. Once your feeders and plants are in place, be patient. It may take the birds days, weeks or even months to locate these new food sources. But, once they do, the feeders will attract more and more birds as time goes on.

You can provide water for the birds with a bird bath, fountain, puddle, or sprinkler. Place it where you can see it from the house and near but not right next to cover where cats may lie in ambush. Make sure the water is shallow enough for the birds to walk and bathe in.

Bird houses are the easiest and most common way to provide nesting sites, but only cavity nesting species use them. By planting appropriate

Yellow Warbler

hedges, shrubs and trees you can create bird habitat on your property, no matter how small it is. You will provide nesting sites for other birds and greatly increase the number of birds around your home. By using these techniques, we have observed nearly 70 species of birds on our property over the past seven years, a number that continues to grow each year.

You can tap into a wealth of information on these and other birding activites by joining local or national groups that include birders, such as the Audubon Society, the National Wildlife Federation, and the American Birding Association. You can also subscribe to various magazines dedicated to birders such as *Birder's World, Wildbird, Bird Watcher's Digest* and *The Living Bird Quarterly.* These organizations and publications can help you learn how to become a responsible birder, a more knowledgeable birder and an involved birder. (See the Suggested References section for addresses.)

Bird Ecology

Birds do not exist in a vacuum but as an integral part of the ecosystem. The ecosystem functions as a whole, with all parts intertwined and working together. Consequently, altering a single strand of this "web of life" affects the entire system. Floods, fires, earthquakes, drought, diseases, insect plagues and other natural events all contribute to a constantly changing balance of nature. In addition, human activites—farming, logging, mining, road building, stream channelization, fire suppression, suburban sprawl, air and water pollution—throw even more variables into the equation. As these factors alter the conditions on a site, the complement of birds living there also changes.

Scientists have identified broad areas—called biomes or life zones—that support similar communities of plants and animals. These regions share similar climates, elevations, soil types and other factors. The central Rockies consist of four life-zones: the alpine tundra, the subalpine forest, the montane forest and the upper Sonoran.

The alpine tundra is easily recognized by its lack of trees. Here, on the mountaintops, the almost constant, bitterly cold winds freeze-dry any vegetation not insulated by a blanket of snow, thus preventing its growth. Consequently, few woody plants grow in the alpine zone and the existing vegetation is primarily low-growing perennials. The first trees growing downslope from the alpine tundra are subalpine fir, white pine and Engelmann spruce. These form the subalpine forest. The montane forest, still lower in elevation, supports Douglas fir, ponderosa pine, quaking aspen and blue spruce. The upper Sonoran life zone, the driest in the region, supports mostly sagebrush, pinyon pine and juniper.

Plant and animal species form a continuum through the life zones. Some birds, such as American robins, have broad environmental requirements and live in all four life zones, so you may see them throughout the region. In contrast, many birds have adapted to survive in only one life zone. Knowing a bird's habitat restrictions can help you identify unfamiliar species. The white-tailed ptarmigan, for example, lives primarily on the alpine tundra. When you see a grouse-like bird in the sagebrush, you can be pretty sure it is not a ptarmigan.

Within a life zone, each species of bird has its own particular way of living—it feeds, nests, moves, and mates in its own unique fashion. While one species of duck feeds in water up to six inches deep, another prefers water from 12 to 24 inches while still another seeks out water from 20 to 40 feet deep. Some ducks eat mostly seeds, others mostly vegetation and still others mostly invertebrates. These individual ways of living are called ecological "niches." The main description section of each writeup gives information on the bird's niche.

Ethics of Birding

Finding food, defending territories, raising young, migrating, escaping predators and seeking shelter from the weather make life tenuous at best for wild birds. In our desire to learn more about birds and enjoy them, we need to use some common sense to avoid disrupting their lives and threatening their survival.

Birds are individuals and have different levels of tolerance. In general, small birds are more tolerant of human disturbance than larger species, but don't rely on this. I have photographed small birds from a distance of a few feet without the aid of a blind without changing their behavior in the slightest. On the other hand, I have had to pull blinds from several hundred feet from a nest when the adults exhibited anxiety and I thought they might abandon their young.

Nesting birds are most susceptible to disturbance early in the nesting cycle. At the egg-laying stage, they may abandon at the slightest disturbance so when you encounter a nest at this stage, leave immediately and watch from a distance. Their attachment to the nest increases through incubation and hatching. Just prior to fledging, some individuals will not leave their young no matter what you do. But, abandonment is not the only problem. Until hatchlings develop feathers, they are incapable of regulating their own body temperature, and the adults must brood the young to keep them warm. If your presence keeps the adults away from the nest too long, the young may be greatly weakened by exposure to even moderate temperatures and in some cases may die—without you having any indication that anything was amiss.

Birding is most enjoyable when the birds can be observed going about their normal activities. Agitation, repeated alarm calls, aggressive behavior or distraction displays are all signs that we are too close. Retreat, or leave if you have to, until the birds calm down. Avoid handling eggs or young, flattening or cutting protective vegetation around nests. These actions increase the likelihood of nest predation by drawing attention to it by scent or simply exposing it to view. Repeatedly flushing birds from favored feeding

Photographing a white-breasted nuthatch. J. L. Wassink

areas can force them to remain in areas with less food and effectively deprive them of needed energy.

Ethical birding is an enjoyable activity and with care, can be carried on with no harmful effects on the birds themselves. Let's make sure we do not destroy the very thing we are seeking to enjoy.

Welcome to the wonderful world of birding!

LOONS (Order Gaviiformes) are large, heavy diving birds. Webbed feet and legs located well back on their bodies make them strong swimmers but render them almost helpless on land. They submerge either by diving forward or by sinking out of sight and may swim 50 to 100 yards underwater before resurfacing. They rarely come ashore except while nesting.

Common Loon   *Gavia immer*

Field marks: 32"; long, flat profile; **black head**; heavy, dagger-like black bill; red eyes; white necklace; **black back densely checkered with small white spots**; yodeling call.

Status: unusual migrant throughout most of the region and RMNP; breeding summer resident in northern Wyoming.

The loon's haunting cry and enchanting behavior seem to embody the spirit of the wilderness. On their way from their wintering areas on the coast to their northern breeding grounds, which extend from northern Wyoming to the Arctic, loons pause to rest and feed on high mountain lakes in the central Rockies. Their distinctive yodel-like wailing laugh is often the first clue to their presence. Upon their arrival in the north, they seek out suitable nesting sites on the shores of lakes containing abundant small fish and crustaceans. Solitude is crucial to their breeding success, and, at present, their numbers appear to be declining primarily due to disturbance of their nesting areas by boaters.

GREBES (Order Podicipediformes) consist of swimming and diving birds with long necks and inconspicuous tails. Legs set well back on their bodies and lobed toes make them excellent swimmers but clumsy walkers. Grebes feed primarily on fish and small aquatic animals. They engage in elaborate courtship displays accompanied by a variety of wails and whistles before building their floating nests of emergent plants in shallow water near shore. Slight differences in bill size distinquish the sexes. Young grebes often ride on their parents' backs, tucked safely under the wing coverts. Sometimes the young remain there even while the adult dives; other times, they pop up like corks soon after the adult submerges.

Pied-billed Grebe   *Podilymbus podiceps*

Field marks: 13"; dull brown, stocky body; **stout, rounded, whitish bill with a black ring**; black bib; white undertail coverts.

Status: fairly common migrant and summer resident of shallow lakes and marshes.

This pond-loving grebe prefers waters with heavy aquatic vegetation, so its presence is often first betrayed by its calls—either whinny-like or a cow call. The specific gravity of a grebe's body is close to that of water, giving it the ability to sink into the water until only its head is exposed and then disappear among the cattails when disturbed. Pied-billed grebes feed heavily on invertebrates and so may frequent ponds that do not contain fish.

Common Loon   T. J. Ulrich

Common Loon with chick   T. J. Ulrich

Pied-billed Grebe   J. L. Wassink

11

Western Grebe   *Aechmophorus occidentalis*

Field marks: 22"; **long, slim, black and white neck;** long, sharp, green-yellow bill; **black cap extends below the eye.**

Status: locally common breeders throughout the region; uncommon migrant in RMNP.

After wintering on the west coast of California, western grebes move inland where they nest in colonies on large, often slightly brackish marshes. Fortunate observers may be able to watch the birds' elaborate courtship display. With heads low and crests erect, the two birds swim toward each other. They dip their beaks into the water and shake their heads vigorously from side to side. Then, they turn sideways, raise upright, arch their wings and necks in a graceful curve and simultaneously rush over the surface of the water. Suddenly they dive, only to reappear seconds later to calmly swim side by side.

Clark's Grebe   *Aechmophorus clarkii*

Field marks: 22"; **long, slim, black and white neck;** long, sharp, orange-yellow bill; **white cheek extends above the eye.**

Status: rare breeder throughout the region.

Once considered by ornithologists to be a separate species, then a color phase of the western grebe, Clark's grebe is once again a separate species. This bird is behaviorally very similar to the western grebe but has a more southerly distribution.

Eared Grebe   *Podiceps nigricollis*

Field marks: 13"; slim shape; short, sharply pointed bill; **black head and neck; golden ear tufts that extend below the eyeline.** The similar horned grebe has a rufous neck and its "horns" do not extend below the eyeline.

Status: fairly common migrant and summer resident except in mountain lakes; rare in RMNP.

Eared grebes nest in colonies on shallow lakes and ponds fringed with cattails or other emergents. They build floating nests in shallow water—often only 8 to 12 inches deep. Unlike the other grebes, they often feed at or near the surface of the water. In contrast to the pied-billed grebes, which escape by disappearing into heavy vegetation, eared grebes head for open water when disturbed. Look for large groups of these very gregarious birds throughout the year.

Western Grebe   J. L. Wassink

Clark's Grebe   J. L. Wassink

Eared Grebe with chick   W. Shattil & R. Rozinski

13

PELICANS AND CORMORANTS (Order Pelecaniformes)

Pelicans (Family Pelecanidae) are large aquatic fish-eating birds with oversized bills and large gular pouches that they use to catch and carry fish. Large feet with webbing between all four toes help propel them through the water.

American White Pelican   *Pelecanus erythrorhynchos*

Field marks: 60"; large size; **large flat bill**; large throat patch; white plumage with black wing tips.

Status: an uncommon migrant and local breeder throughout the area; migrant only in RMNP.

With wings spanning 9½ feet, American white pelicans are the largest birds in the central Rockies. Primarily fish eaters, they feed while swimming on the surface of the water by submerging their heads and scooping up fish in their large bills. The large gular pouch expands to contain the catch and up to three gallons of water. They press their pouch against their throat to expel the water and then swallow the fish. Groups of pelicans may fish cooperatively by forming a line and herding fish into shallow water. The birds nest in colonies on isolated islands in large lakes or reservoirs such as Antelope Island in the Great Salt Lake of Utah. Newly hatched young feed on regurgitated "soup." Older youngsters reach into the adult's gullet for partially digested fish. The birds leave the nesting colony for their feeding grounds, which may be more than fifty miles away, in orderly lines, flying low over the water.

Cormorants (Family Phalacrocoracidae) are heavy bodied, primarily black birds that swim low in the water with their bill tilted upward. They dive from the surface, sometimes to depths of several hundred feet, and swim underwater in pursuit of fish. They have gular pouches similar to, but much smaller than those of the pelicans. The sharply hooked bill enables them to grasp and hold their slippery prey.

Double-crested Cormorant   *Phalacrocorax auritus*

Field marks: 29"; long, low profile on the water; **uplifted head**; hooked bill; orange-yellow throat patch; **glossy black plumage**.

Status: fairly common summer resident except in the high mountain lakes where it is a migrant only; uncommon migrant in RMNP.

The only species of cormorant that ventures inland and so the only cormorant likely to be seen in the central Rockies, double-crested cormorants are excellent fisherman. Surprisingly, their plumage is not waterproof and they often perch with their wings half open, drying their feathers. They nest in mixed colonies, often with great blue herons, on rocky islands or in trees near large lakes or reservoirs.

American White Pelican   J. L. Wassink

American White Pelican   J. L. Wassink
Double-crested Cormorant   J. L. Wassink

15

EGRETS, HERONS, BITTERNS AND IBIS
(Order Ciconiiformes)

Egrets, Herons and Bitterns (Family Ardeidae) are long legged wading birds with long necks and long, straight, dagger-like bills. Most nest in colonies and develop long plumes or aigrettes during the breeding season. They fly with deliberate wingbeats, heads drawn back and legs extended.

Snowy Egret   *Egretta thula*

Field marks: 24"; small size; white plumage; **black bill; black legs; yellow feet**; plumed head during the breeding season.

Status: fairly common migrant and local breeder throughout the region.

These small agile egrets prefer shallow marshes where they often join other herons. Active feeders, they stir the bottom muck with one golden foot and then use their sharp bill to nab the small fish and crustaceans they disturb. Other times, they may wait quietly in ambush, stalk slowly through the shallows, or even venture to the uplands in pursuit of grasshoppers and other insects. At one time, snowy egrets were almost exterminated by plume hunters who sought the long aigrettes that develop during the breeding season.

Cattle Egret   *Bubulcus ibis*

Field marks: 20"; small size; white plumage; **yellow bill; yellow-pink legs and feet**; buffy-orange crest, breast and back during breeding season.

Status: uncommon but breeding populations are becoming established in the region.

An Old World bird, cattle egrets first appeared in the southeastern United States in 1952. From there, they rapidly worked their way north and west and reached this region several years ago. Not bound to wetlands as strongly as the other herons and egrets, the cattle egret often accompanies livestock in dry pastures. There, they feed on the insects and other small animals disturbed by the grazing animals.

Great Blue Heron   *Ardea herodias*

Field marks: 52"; **large size**; long yellow bill; **bluish-gray color**; black crown stripe and crest.

Status: resident throughout much of the region except in the high mountains; migrant in RMNP.

The largest and most visible herons in the area, great blue herons frequent the shores of shallow waters. They may stand motionless until an unsuspecting fish, frog or snake ventures by. Or, they may stalk slowly through the shallows, always ready to skewer any creature small enough for them to swallow. Where suitable trees are available, they nest in loose colonies well up in cottonwood trees. In other areas, they nest on the ground on isolated islands.

16

Snowy Egret   J. L. Wassink

Cattle Egret   J. L. Wassink

Great Blue Heron   J. L. Wassink

Great Blue Heron   J. L. Wassink

Black-crowned Night Heron · · · · · · · · · · · · *Nycticorax nycticorax*

Field marks: 25"; **small stocky shape; black crown and back**; red eyes; grayish sides and breast; short legs; immatures are heavily streaked, brownish-gray.

Status: rare migrant in the high mountains, a fairly common summer resident in the lower elevations; rare in RMNP.

Except when they are feeding young, which is a full-time job, night herons work the night shift, taking over the prime feeding areas at dusk when the other herons are returning to their night roosts. Large eyes enable them to see in the dim light as they stalk slowly through the shallows in pursuit of frogs and small crustaceans, which they dispatch with a lightning quick strike from their dagger-like bill. The night heron also fishes from ambush.

American Bittern · · · · · · · · · · · · · · · · · · *Botaurus lentiginosus*

Field marks: 25"; stocky shape; moderate size; **black neck stripe; brown streaked plumage**.

Status: fairly common summer resident in the region and in RMNP.

This secretive marsh and bog dweller frequents the heavy vegetation bordering beaver ponds and marshes. Unlike the other herons, which feed mostly in open water, the solitary bittern prefers to feed among rushes. When startled, it freezes—neck and beak extended skyward, streaked breast blending beautifully with the surrounding rushes—and seems to disappear before your eyes. Although difficult to see, it is easy to hear. Its unmistakable call, a loud, low pumping noise, seems to reverberate through the marsh.

Ibis (Family *Threskiornithidae)* are separated from the herons and egrets by their thin, decurved or flat spoon-shaped bills. In addition, their wingbeats are rapid, and they fly with their necks extended. Ibis move about actively in pursuit of food and often nest in mixed colonies with herons and egrets.

White-faced Ibis · · · · · · · · · · · · · · · · · · · *Plegadis falcinellus*

Field marks: 23"; heron-like profile but with **down-curved bill; dark, bronze iridescent plumage**; white line around bill and eye during breeding season.

Status: uncommon migrant and local summer resident throughout the region; rare in RMNP.

Ibis feed by stalking. Moving slowly through the shallow marshes, they probe for insects, small fish, small frogs, tadpoles, invertebrates and earthworms, which they eagerly snap up. Ibis build grass-lined nests from dead reeds and twigs and place them in tall reeds, on floating vegetation or on small islands. Both parents help incubate and subsequently feed the dull-black, downy young.

Black-crowned Night Heron
J. L. Wassink

American Bittern   J. L. Wassink

White-faced Ibis   J. L. Wassink

White-faced Ibis   J. L. Wassink

SWANS, GEESE AND DUCKS (Order Anseriformes)

Waterfowl (Family Anatidae) are well-suited to spending most of their lives on water. Their flat bodies increase bouyancy and their fluffy down insulation wards off the chill of cold water. Long necks allow them to reach deep into the water to feed and their flattened bills, equipped with tooth-like edges called lamellae, enable them to strain tiny food items from the water. Short powerful legs and webs between the three front toes propel them through the water. And, when the lakes in the north begin to freeze, their narrow pointed wings carry them to warmer climes far to the south. The young are covered with down and leave the nest soon after hatching.

Swans (Tribe Cygninae), with their pure white plumage, large size and long necks, are by far the most impressive of the waterfowl. Swans feed on submerged plants by dipping their head and neck in shallow water. Birds living in areas with high concentrations of dissolved iron in the water often have rust stains on their heads and upper necks. The male (cob) and the female (pen) mate for life and usually raise two young (cygnets) each year.

Trumpeter Swan   *Cygnus buccinator*

Field marks: 65"; large size; white plumage; black bill; **best distinquished from the tundra swan by its resonant call.**

Status: permanent resident in northwest Wyoming and eastern Idaho.

Between 1853 and 1877, Hudson's Bay Company handled more than 17,000 swan skins, a good portion of them trumpeters. The company sold these skins in London markets for adornments and for use in powder puffs and down garments. This extensive hunting continued until 1933, when only 69 trumpeter swans were believed to exist in the lower 48 states—all in the Yellowstone area. The establishment of the Red Rock Lakes National Wildlife Refuge in 1935, which has an abundance of the shallow, calm and slow-moving water the trumpeter prefers, protected the breeding habitat of these magnificent birds. The population slowly increased until the 1950s, when it reached about 600 birds. Since then, transplants to other areas have helped reestablish populations of trumpeter swans elsewhere in the lower forty-eight.

Tundra Swan   *Cygnus columbianus*

Field marks: 53"; large size; white plumage; black bill, often with **a yellow spot in front of the eye**; distinguished from trumpeter swan by voice—**call of tundra swan is a high pitched yelp.**

Status: uncommon migrant throughout the area; rare in RMNP.

Among the earliest spring migrants, large flocks of tundra swans stop over at favored feeding spots such as the marshy margins of the Great Salt Lake in Utah and other areas throughout the region on their way north to breed on the arctic tundra. Recently renamed tundra swans, to reflect their breeding grounds, these birds were formerly called whistling swans, for the sound made by their powerful wings during flight.

Trumpeter Swan with cygnet

Trumpeter Swan

Tundra Swan .

Geese *(Tribe Anserinae)* are intermediate in size, weight and neck length between the swans and the ducks. Like the swans, the sexes are similar, mate for life and share domestic responsibilities. With legs set farther forward on their bodies than either the swans or the ducks, they are more mobile on land than those birds and do more grazing and feeding on waste grain. Geese migrate in noisy flocks that are difficult to ignore.

Canada Goose   *Branta canadensis*

> **Field marks:** 36"; **black head and neck; white cheek patch**; brownish back and sides.
>
> **Status:** very common resident breeder throughout the area; migrant only in RMNP.

The wedge-shaped skeins of "honkers" that grace the autumn skies are known the country over as a sure sign of fall. Canada geese are extremely adaptable birds, a characteristic that has made them the best known and most widely distributed goose in North America. Their ability to nest anywhere they can find a site relatively protected from predators—on cliffs, in osprey nests, on small islands, atop muskrat mounds and in a variety of man-made nesting structures—has made it possible to introduce breeding populations to many new areas. After the breeding season, the family groups come together in large flocks and spend their nights resting on large rivers, lakes and reservoirs. At dawn, they leave the protection of the water and venture out into nearby fields to graze or feed on waste grain. At dusk, they once again seek the protection of the water. Canada geese mate for life and both parents aid in raising the young. Migrating flocks of these birds, which arrive noisily in line or wedge formations, join resident populations in spring and fall.

Snow Goose   *Chen caerulescens*

> **Field marks:** 29"; small size; **all white plumage; rosy pink bill with a black "grin patch"**; black wing tips; also a less common "blue" phase that has a white head and neck and a dark grayish body.
>
> **Status:** uncommon migrant throughout the area; rare in RMNP.

Snow geese winter in the marshes along the Gulf coast and in the valleys of central California and only pass through this area on their way to and from their breeding grounds in northern Canada. The noisiest of the geese, snow geese gather on large marshes where the din of their calls can be heard at great distances. They feed on seeds, root stalks and tubers. Like the swans, their heads and upper necks may become stained by iron-rich water.

Canada Goose J. L. Wassink

Snow Goose J. L. Wassink

Snow Goose, "blue phase." J. L. Wassink

Surface Ducks (Tribe Anatinae), like the swans and geese, feed from the surface of the water by tipping. Limited by their smaller size and shorter necks, they cannot reach as deep into the water as the larger birds and consequently frequent shallow water. Unlike the larger birds, ducks are dimorphic—the male being the larger and more colorful of the pair, the female appearing nondescript. Although experienced birders can easily identify the females, beginners can best recognize them by the company they keep. Both sexes sport a bright patch of color, called a speculum, on their secondary flight feathers. Instead of requiring a running start like the rest of the waterfowl, surface ducks leap vertically into the air from the surface of the water. Vegetarians throughout most of the year, they add small molluscs, insects, insect larvae, a variety of other small invertebrates and small fish to their diet during the nesting season.

Mallard   *Anas platyrhynchos*

Field marks: 16"; *male*-**green head**; white neck ring; chestnut breast; blue speculum; *female*-mottled brown color; **yellowish bill**; blue speculum; whitish tail.

Status: Abundant permanent resident throughout the area and in RMNP.

The mallard is the most abundant and most familiar duck in North America. The ancestor of most domestic ducks, the highly adaptable mallard makes itself at home wherever it finds suitable shallow water. Hardy birds, mallards can endure fierce cold, needing only open water and food to survive. Where some degree of protection accompanies suitable habitat, such as in city parks and other preserves, populations can expand to the point of becoming a problem.

Like other dabbling ducks, mallards feed on the surface of shallow water or on the bottom by "tipping" up in the water. They may, however, make occasional shallow dives to reach tidbits in slightly deeper water.

Mating pairs begin bonding in late fall and continue through the winter, with most birds already paired by the time they arrive here in the spring. The pair establishes a home range that includes one or more waiting sites, strips of bare shore surrounded by standing vegetation, which they defend against other pairs of mallards. The pair flies reconnaissance over the surrounding land, probably to choose a nesting site. Once the pair builds the nest, the female begins laying her eggs. As she spends less and less time at the waiting area, the pair bond begins to dissolve. Eventually, the drake joins other drakes in a nearby marsh where they undergo their annual molt, leaving the female to incubate and raise the brood on her own.

Since the female does not begin incubation until the entire clutch is laid, the ducklings usually hatch within hours of each other. Almost before they are dry, the hen uses her characteristic "quack" to lead them to the water's edge where she teaches them to catch insects and invertebrates. The young continue to grow and mature and leave the family unit before fall.

Mallard
J. L. Wassink

Mallard hen with ducklings
J. L. Wassink

Mallard, "grunt-whistle" display
J. L. Wassink

Gadwall
Anas strepera

Field marks: 20"; *male*-**gray plumage; black rump**; white speculum; *female*-mottled brown plumage; unspotted orange bill; white speculum.

Status: abundant migrant and fairly common resident throughout the area, especially at the lower elevations; summer resident but no confirmed nesting in RMNP.

Not as colorful as many of the other ducks, gadwalls are easily overlooked. They tend to dive more than the other dabbling ducks and prefer stagnant sloughs where they feed on aquatic vegetation. Excellent walkers, gadwalls often feed on mast, weed seeds and waste grain in woodlands and grainfields. Populations of gadwall seem to be increasing as they gradually extend their range eastward from the western states.

Northern Pintail
Anas acuta

Field marks: 25"; slim shape; *male*-brown head; **vertical white chest and neck stripe; long pointed tail**; black rump; *female*-brown color; long neck; long tail.

Status: abundant migrant and fairly common breeding resident throughout the region; migrant in RMNP.

As very early migrants, tight flocks of these long, slender, graceful fliers can be seen wheeling and gliding over marshes or grain fields. They often feed on dry land and may nest well away from the water. When feeding in water, their long necks allow them to reach greater depths, and so they do less "tipping" than the other surface ducks. Northern pintails head back south before the hot days of summer are over—leaving the central Rockies in August. They are one of the most abundant North American ducks, outnumbered only by the mallard and possibly the lesser scaup.

Gadwall

J. L. Wassink

Northern Pintail drake

J. L. Wassink

Northern Pintail hen

J. L. Wassink

American Wigeon
Anas americana

Field marks: 19"; *male*-**white crown; green eye patch**; brown back; green speculum; black rump; **white upper wing coverts** visible in flight; *female*-streaked brown body; black speculum; white upper wing coverts visible in flight.

Status: abundant migrant and rare to common summer resident throughout the lower elevations of the region; rare migrant in RMNP.

More vegetarian than the other ducks, wigeon prefer open marshes and lakes with aquatic vegetation near the surface. "Baldpate" are social ducks and often associate with gadwalls. Prior to nesting, spring courtship brings sharp whistling calls and frequent aerial chases. In winter, wigeon keep company with large rafts of diving ducks. There, in addition to seeking out their own food, wigeon engage in piracy. While the divers go down after tasty morsels, the wigeon wait on the surface. When a diver surfaces with a tasty tidbit, one of the wigeon grabs the morsel, eats it and waits for another opportunity to pirate another tidbit.

Eurasian Wigeon
Anas penelope

Field marks: 18"; *male*-**cream-colored forehead**; rusty brown head; gray flanks; *female*-similar to the female American wigeon.

Status: rare migrant throughout the region; has not been seen in RMNP.

Common in Europe, these birds usually visit this country as lone birds in flocks of American wigeon. Although they are seen frequently, especially along the coasts, there are no records of them breeding in this country. The habits and ecology of the European wigeon are vitually identical to that of the American wigeon.

Northern Shoveler
Anas clypeata

Field marks: 19"; *male*-**large spatulate bill; green head**; rusty sides; white chest; pale blue upper wing coverts; *female*-large spatulate bill; mottled brown coloration.

Status: abundant migrant and common to uncommon summer resident in the lower elevations throughout the region; rare in upper elevations and in RMNP.

Shovelers feed on tiny invertebrates in very shallow water. Taking a billfull of bottom ooze, the "spoonbill" swishes his bill from side to side, forcing out water and liquid mud between the comb-like lamellae on the edges of the bill and leaving behind insect larvae, small crustaceans, seeds and bits of plant material. Or, he may just swim slowly, with his neck extended, and use his bill to skim insects off the surface of the water. If suitable shallows are not available, shovelers will also tip to feed like the other surface ducks.

American Wigeon J. L. Wassink

Eurasian Wigeon J. L. Wassink
Northern Shoveler J. L. Wassink

Blue-winged Teal   *Anas discors*

Field marks: 15"; *male*-**small size**; slate-gray head; **white crescent in front of eye**; green speculum; **pale blue upper wing coverts**; *female*-brown plumage; pale spot behind bill; pale blue upper wing coverts.

Status: abundant migrant and fairly common summer resident throughout most of the area and in RMNP.

Long distance migrants, wintering as far away as Central America, blue-winged teal are one of the last ducks to arrive in spring and the first to head south in autumn. Upon arrival, they seek out small shallow marshes where they stick close to shore, feeding on aquatic plants in the shallows and resting on the shore. These skilled fliers resemble squadrons of fighter planes on maneuvers as they fly in tight formation, just above the marsh vegetation.

Cinnamon Teal   *Anas cyanoptera*

Field marks: 15"; *male*-small size; **cinnamon-colored plumage**; red eyes; **pale blue upper wing coverts**;*female*-brown plumage; large broad bill; no whitish spot behind bill like the female blue-winged teal.

Status: rare to common migrant and fairly common summer resident throughout the area; vagrant only in RMNP

Most abundant in the marshes and wetlands surrounding the Great Salt Lake in Utah, the cinnamon teal rarely ventures east of the Great Plains. Like the blue-winged teal, the cinnamon teal prefers small shallow marshes. But, they tend to choose drier and/or more alkaline areas than the blue-winged teal and replace them in these habitats. Cinnamon teal usually form smaller flocks than the other teal. They feed on aquatic plants in shallow water, along the water's edge or on mudflats and nest on land, hidden in dense vegetation.

Green-winged Teal   Anas crecca

Field marks: 14"; *male*-small size; **chestnut head with a green patch from the eye to the nape; white vertical stripe up side of breast**; *female*-brown plumage; white belly; green speculum.

Status: abundant migrant and fairly common summer resident throughout the area; rare in RMNP.

After wintering in the Gulf States and Mexico, the green-winged teal is the first teal to arrive on its breeding grounds here in the central Rockies and into Canada. The smallest of the North American dabbling ducks, these agile birds fly swiftly in flocks, wheeling and dipping over the small ponds they often frequent. The female builds her nest in tall vegetation near the water and lays ten to twelve eggs.

Pair of Blue-winged Teal

Cinnamon Teal drake

Green-winged Teal drake

Bay Ducks or Diving Ducks (Tribe Aythyinae), as the two designations imply, are ducks that prefer the open water of fairly large, deep rivers, lakes and reservoirs and feed by diving. They winter along the coastal bays on both coasts and the Gulf of Mexico, but move to inland marshes in spring to nest. Unlike the surface ducks which build their nests on land, divers build their nests over water. Diving ducks take flight by running across the surface of the water until they gain enough momentum to become airborne. Their larger feet, lobed hind toe, and legs set farther back on their bodies make them more powerful swimmers than the surface ducks but more awkward on land.

Redhead   *Aythya americana*

Field marks: 19"; *male*-**rusty red head; dish-faced profile**; black breast and rump; gray back and sides; *female*-brown plumag; round head; white belly.

Status: abundant migrant and fairly common summer resident throughout most of the region; migrant only in RMNP.

Look for redheads all across the region in the spring as they arrive in fast-moving V's to rest and feed on their way north to the prairie potholes of Montana, the Dakotas and Canada where most of them breed. Although most of them move on, enough of them stay and breed to make the redhead the most common nesting diver in the central Rockies. Draining of nesting ponds has permanently reduced the numbers of these as well as other pothole nesting ducks. Redhead females appear to be rather careless with their eggs—often laying them in the nests of other species or constructing "dump" nests where several redhead females lay eggs but do not incubate them. The females also build their own nests and raise a clutch of their own. More vegetarian than other divers, redheads like shallow lakes and marshes where they dive to depths of around 10 feet in pursuit of pondweed, their favorite food.

Canvasback   *Aythya valisineria*

Field marks: 20"; *male*-**long sloping forehead**; chestnut red head; **white back and sides**; *female*-long sloping forehead; brown plumage.

Status: common migrant but rare breeder throughout the region, including RMNP.

One of the largest diving ducks, "cans," as they are affectionately called by hunters, are largely vegetarian. Capable of diving to depths of 30 feet, they most often feed on the tuberous roots of aquatic plants growing in 3 to 15 feet of water. Favored foods are wapatoo and pondweed. After breeding in the emergent vegetation surrounding small ponds and lakes, canvasbacks congregate in great numbers on large lakes and reservoirs. Long pointed wings carry these powerful fliers at speeds of up to 60 miles per hour. Like many of the pothole nesting ducks, canvasbacks do not breed in drought years when their nesting ponds dry up.

Redhead drake and hen   J. L. Wassink

Canvasback drake   J. L. Wassink

Canvasback hen   T. J. Ulrich

33

Ring-necked Duck   *Aythya collaris*

Field marks: 12"; *male*-**dark head, neck and breast** with purple sheen; **white band on bill**; black back; gray sides; *female*-gray/brown plumage; gray bill with black tip and white ring; pale eye-ring; steep forehead; peaked crown.

Status: uncommon migrant and rare breeder in the area; migrant only in RMNP.

Woodland ponds ringed with stubbly growth provide the preferred habitat of the ring-necked duck. These ducks build their nests in boggy or marshy areas rather than on dry land. Although they can dive to 40 feet, they prefer to feed in water from 2 to 5 feet deep where they hunt for tubers, pondweed and seeds. In even shallower water, they will "tip" like the dabblers. Migrants only in this region, ring-necked ducks pass through late in the spring on their way to the reedy borders of bogs and ponds of northern Canada. Very gregarious ducks, they form sizable flocks during migration and then gather on large lakes and tidal estuaries to spend the winter.

Lesser Scaup   *Aythya affinis*

Field marks: 16"; *male*-dark head, neck and breast with a purple sheen; **peaked head profile**; barred gray back and sides; black rump; *female*-brown plumage.

Status: abundant migrant and rare breeder throughout the area; migrant in RMNP.

Lesser scaup pass through the central Rockies early in the spring on their way to their breeding grounds in Montana, the Dakotas and Canada. They congregate in the deep water of large reservoirs and lakes where they feed almost exclusively on aquatic invertebrates. Nicknamed "blue bills," scaup are expert divers. In fall, they linger in the north until forced to move south when the lakes begin to freeze.The greater scaup is similar but lacks a peaked head profile, often has a green sheen to the dark head and appears whiter on the body. The greater scaup nests farther north than the lesser scaup, nesting only in northern Canada. Scaup nest late and their young often do not hatch until July. Both scaup winter in large rafts in coastal bays while the lesser can also be found on inland waters near the coasts.

Ring-necked Duck drake   T. J. Ulrich

Lesser Scaup drake   J. L. Wassink

Lesser Scaup hen   T. J. Ulrich

35

Common Goldeneye
Bucephela clangula

Field marks: 18"; *male*-green gloss on head; **yellow eye; white, round face spot**; mostly white body; *female*-mostly gray body; brown head; **yellow eye.**

Status: common migrant and winter resident in the southern part of the area and in RMNP; more common in the northern part of the region.

The last migrants to retreat to the south in the fall, common goldeneye remain throughout the winter on the open water of large reservoirs or rivers. Their swift flight produces a whistling sound—thus the nickname "whistler." When the nesting season approaches, these cavity nesters choose forested habitat where large trees provide the necessary hollows. After hatching, the chicks launch themselves into the air and bounce unhurt off the ground.

Barrow's Goldeneye
Bucephala islandica

Field marks: 18"; *male*-purple gloss on head; **crescent-shaped face spot**; more black on the sides than common goldeneye; *female*-similar to the common goldeneye female but with an all-yellow bill.

Status: a common breeder in northwestern Wyoming; an uncommon migrant throughout the rest of the region and in RMNP.

The Barrow's goldeneye has a slightly more northern distribution than the common goldeneye and winters as far north as it can find open water. Like the common goldeneye, these birds nest in tree cavities near mountain lakes, ponds and rivers. They eat mostly small fish although they will also take some invertebrates and bits of vegetation.

Bufflehead
Bucephala albeola

Field marks: 14"; *male*-**small size**; mostly white plumage; dark iridescent head with a **wedge-shaped white patch**; *female*-small size; gray-brown plumage; **light patch below and behind the eye.**

Status: local breeding residents in northwest Wyoming and nearby Idaho; migrants and winter residents elsewhere; rare migrant in RMNP.

The smallest of the divers, the diminutive bufflehead is a perky little duck that almost seems to "bounce." Unlike the other diving ducks, it can leap directly out of the water like a puddle duck when disturbed. The female usually selects an old flicker hole, often in a live aspen, in which to lay her eggs. Upon hatching, the young have only one way to reach the ground—jump—which they do and land unharmed. Like most of the ducks, buffleheads winter in waters all along the Pacific coast and the Gulf of Mexico.

Common Goldeneye drake   J. L. Wassink

Barrow's Goldeneye drake   T. J. Ulrich

Bufflehead drake   J. L. Wassink

37

Ruddy Duck
Oxyura jamaicensis

Field marks: 15"; *male*-deep rust-red body; **bright blue bill**; black cap; white cheeks; **long tail often carried pointed straight up**; *female*-brownish color; whitish cheek patch; long, often upturned tail.

Status: common to abundant migrant; fairly common summer resident throughout the region; rare migrant in RMNP.

Most common at lower elevations, ruddy ducks breed in shallow marshes overgrown with vegetation and ringed with cattails or bulrushes. There the male performs his unique courtship routine of thumping his bill on his breast and producing a thumping-gurgling sound. The females lay unusually large eggs and frequently drop them in the nests of other ducks—a habit that is yet to be explained by scientists. Like most of the diving ducks, ruddys winter in coastal bays.

Common Merganser
Mergus merganser

Field marks: 24"; *male*-long, low profile; black above, white below; **green head; long, slender, hooked red bill**; red legs; *female*-dark chestnut head; gray plumage; clear white throat.

Status: common migrant and resident throughout the area and in RMNP.

One of the earliest to go north, common mergansers reach their nesting grounds as the ice is melting. They prefer boreal forests near streams or marshy bays with abundant small fishes and nest in hollow trees or similarly well-protected cavities. This very adept swimmer feeds almost exclusively on fish, locating prey either by swimming with only its bill and eyes submerged or by diving. The common merganser captures its meal in its slender saw-toothed bill—earning the nickname "sawbill." When flushed, it must make a long exhausting run across the surface of the water to gain enough speed to become airborne. The similar red-breasted merganser has a more northerly distribution, frequents salt water more often, has a wispy crest, a white neck and a reddish breast.

Ruddy Duck drake T. J. Ulrich

Common Merganser drake J. L. Wassink

Common Merganser hen J. L. Wassink

VULTURES, HAWKS, EAGLES AND FALCONS (Order
Falconiformes) feed on flesh. Most of these birds have strong legs and feet
tipped with long, curved talons for grasping and killing live prey and strong,
heavy, hooked beaks for tearing the prey into bite-sized pieces. A few
members of this family are scavengers. In most species, the females are
generally larger but otherwise similar to the males.

Vultures (Family Cathartidae) use their broad wings to soar effortlessly
for hours on rising thermals. These large blackish birds lead a scavenger's
life, and their naked heads do not get as dirty as a feathered head would.

Turkey Vulture   *Cathartes aura*

Field marks: 29"; black body; small naked reddish head; *in flight*-**uptilted
wings**; wings black in front, gray behind.

Status: Fairly common summer resident throughout the area and in
RMNP.

Look for turkey vultures circling effortlessly on uptilted wings as they
ride rising thermals high overhead. Scavengers with keen eyes and a well-
developed sense of smell, vultures locate carrion either by sight or smell.
Almost as soon as the first big black bird drops from the sky, more seem to
appear out of nowhere to share the meal. More common at elevations below
9,000 feet, they nest in crevices or under overhangs on inaccessible cliffs.
There, they feed their one or two youngsters on regurgitated carrion.

Hawks and Eagles (Family Accipitridae) are all excellent fliers with
strong legs and powerful talons. They lack the characteristic notch in the
beak common to the falcons.

Osprey   *Pandion haliaetus*

Field marks: 24"; predominantly white; broad black cheek line; black
back; *in flight*-long white wings bent at the "wrist"; **black "wrist"
markings**.

Status: uncommon summer resident in the southern part of the region;
more common from west central to northwest Wyoming and nearby Idaho.

Osprey live along clear mountain lakes and streams where fish are
plentiful. They spot fish from the air, then "dive" foot-first into the water to
nab their catch. A reversible outer toe and spiny pads (called spicules) on the
bottoms of their feet give them a better grip on their slippery prey. The
osprey carries the fish, with the head turned forward, either to a perch to eat
it or to the nest to feed the young. These "fish hawks" build bulky nests near
water in tall trees, on power poles or, more recently, on nesting platforms
provided by concerned utility companies. Ospreys will use the same nests
year after year. Once decimated by DDT, populations of these birds are
increasing once again.

Turkey Vulture   J. L. Wassink

Osprey   J. L. Wassink

Osprey   J. L. Wassink

41

Accipiters are small to medium hawks that hunt in heavy woodlands and feed mainly on birds. Their short rounded wings and long tails give them the speed and maneuverability they need when pursuing small birds through dense woods. In open flight, they alternate flapping and gliding. Females are generally larger than the males.

Sharp-shinned Hawk   *Accipiter striatus*

Field marks: *male*-11"; *female*-13"; small size; short, rounded wings; long, **square-tipped tail**; dark gray above; white with rust bars below.
Status: uncommon resident throughout the area and in RMNP.

The sharp-shinned hawk is the smallest and most common of the three North American accipiter hawks. It hunts by flashing through the trees, flushing its prey, and then snatching the fleeing victim out of midair. Occasionally, the hawk will be so intent on pursuing its prey that it will crash headlong into a thicket or tree branch. Once caught the prey is taken to a favorite perch, plucked and eaten. Sharp-shinned hawks also take some insects and small mammals, usually mice.

Northern Harrier   *Circus cyaneus*

Field marks: *male*-18"; slim shape; **silvery gray**; *female*-22"; slim; **dark brown**; *in flight*-long, narrow, uplifted wings; white rump; flies low over the ground; sometimes hovers.
Status: fairly common throughout the region; common summer resident in RMNP.

Look for "marsh hawks" flying buoyantly through open country—usually quartering low over marshy habitat in search of mice, voles, frogs or snakes. Facial disks, similar to those of the owls, focus sound and enable them to locate prey by sound as well as by sight—a useful ability in the tall grass habitat they patrol. Northern harriers nest in marshes, building their nests just above the water. The male brings food to the female during incubation and early during the brooding. The female, always alert, sees him coming and leaves the nest to meet him. He drops the food item which she catches in midair and immediately returns to the nest. Marsh hawks move south for the winter, spending the cold months from the southern part of this region down to South America.

Sharp-shinned Hawk   J. L. Wassink

Immature Northern Harrier at nest   J. L. Wassink

Male Northern Harrier   T. J. Ulrich

43

Buteos are medium to large soaring hawks that frequent open country. Consequently, their wings are broad and round and their tails are broad and fan-shaped. Buteos locate their prey from high overhead and then pursue it from a steep dive. Several of these species have two color phases, one dark and one light, which complicates identification.

Ferruginous Hawk
Buteo regalis

Field marks: 25"; *light phase*-light head; **dark legs form V against light belly**; tail light and unbanded; primary feathers light and black tipped; *dark phase*-head lighter than back; tail light and unbanded; primary feathers light and black-tipped; dark chest, underwing covert and legs.

Status: uncommon hawk throughout the region; rare in RMNP.

These large, mild-mannered hawks frequent open habitats where they hunt from the ground, from a perch or while soaring. Ferruginous hawks eat a variety of prey, including rodents, insects, snakes and birds, but prefer ground squirrels, when available. They nest almost anywhere—power structures, on ledges of buttes and cliffs, in ground nests on appropriate hillsides and, more recently, on nesting structures provided for them by biologists.

Red-tailed Hawk
Buteo jamaicensis

Field marks: 23"; *in flight*-**rusty tail**; long broad wings; wings whitish except for dark leading edge from body to wrist; round tail; *perched*-white breast; dark head and back.

Status: fairly common resident throughout the area and in RMNP.

Its adaptability has made the red-tailed hawk the most common hawk in the region. It feeds primarily on rodents and rabbits but will also take birds, snakes, frogs and virtually anything else of appropriate size that it can catch—even rattlesnakes. This raptor usually nests in large trees but, in more open country, will nest on cliffs. Red-tailed hawks winter in the southern states along the Gulf of Mexico but return to the same nest year after year. Because of its predatory habits, it has suffered from persecution by humans intent on protecting their domestic animals.

Swainson's Hawk
Buteo swainsoni

Field marks: 21"; *dark phase*-dark head, back, primaries, chest and belly; long tail is finely barred and has a broad terminal band; *light phase*-**dark head and back; dark chest band**; finely barred long tail has a broad terminal band.

Status: fairly common summer resident throughout the CR and in RMNP.

Tame and unaggressive for a hawk, Swainson's hawks hunt from an elevated perch on a roadside fencepost or by soaring over the meadows with wings in a slight V. They prey on ground squirrels, rabbits, grasshoppers, frogs, lizards and snakes and a few small birds. Swainson's hawks build their flimsy stick nests in trees or on cliffs and normally raise two young each year. They spend their winters in Argentina—a round trip of 11,000 to 17,000 miles—making them the champion travelers among the hawks.

Ferruginous Hawk
W. Shattil & R. Rozinski

Red-tailed Hawk
W. Shattil & R. Rosinski

Swainson's Hawk
E. T. Jones

Swainson's Hawk, dark phase
E. T. Jones

Golden Eagle

Aquila chrysaetos

Field marks: 35"; *adults*-**large size**; dark plumage; **golden cast to hind neck**; fully feathered tarsus; *in flight*-large size; dark plumage; large, broad wings; *immature*-dark plumage with some white spots; *in flight*-dark plumage; white "wrist" spots; white in tail but tip black.

Status: fairly common resident throughout the area and in RMNP.

The largest raptor in the central Rockies, the golden eagle is a bird of the mountains. It prefers open country—alpine meadows, mountain ridges, grasslands, sagebrush plateaus, pinyon-juniper slopes and semi-desert canyons. For prey, it seems to prefer mammals, such as ground squirrels, rabbits and marmots, but will also take birds such as ring-necked pheasants and chukars. Some accuse golden eagles of stealing lambs, which they do in rare instances but not with any regularity. Like the other raptors, persecution by humans, pesticide contamination and elimination of its prey by habitat alteration are the main factors limiting its populations. Golden eagles mate for life, nest in trees or on cliffs and raise one or two chicks per year.

Bald Eagle

Haliaeetus leucocephalus

Field marks: 36"; *adults*-dark plumage; **white head and tail; heavy yellow bill**; *immature*-dark plumage; *in flight*-underwing coverts lighter than flight feathers.

Status: rare resident in the southern parts of the region and in RMNP; more common breeder farther north.

Our national symbol, the bald eagle feeds mostly on fish, waterfowl and carrion. It nests near fertile lakes and rivers that support an abundance of non-game fish such as suckers and squawfish, which it snatches from the surface of the water with its sharp talons. Bald eagles also feed on waterfowl, rodents and carrion found near water. Not above piracy, they will harry a fish-laden osprey into dropping its booty, which the eagle snags out of midair. Nests are usually in tall trees near water. Bald eagles pair for life and return to the same territory year after year. Pair bonds are renewed each year with spectacular courtship displays, including locked-talon cartwheels that begin high in the air and spin toward the earth with breathtaking speed. The pair raises two young each year if the food supply is sufficient. Threatened by DDT contamination of its food supply, bald eagles seem to be recovering. The white head of the adult bird appears at about three to five years of age.

Golden Eagle   W. Shattil & R. Rozinski

Golden Eagle   T. J. Ulrich

Immature Bald Eagle   T. J. Ulrich

Adult Bald Eagle   T. J. Ulrich

47

Falcons (Family Falconidae), with their notched beaks, long pointed wings and long slender tails are strong, fast fliers. These streamlined birds inhabit open country and locate their prey from a prominent perch or from a vantage point high in the air and overtake it by means of a long steep dive.

Prairie Falcon   *Falco mexicanus*

> **Field marks:** 16"; medium size; pale brown above; light below in flight; pointed wings; quick wingbeats; **black "armpits."**
> **Status:** uncommon summer resident in areas with cliffs near open country; more common in winter in southern parts of the region; resident in RMNP.

Prairie falcons inhabit the dry sagebrush-covered semi-desert flats and plains. They hunt mainly ground squirrels. After spotting their prey, the prairie falcon "stoops," or dives, at speeds approaching 200 miles per hour. They build no nest, merely laying their eggs in a "scrape" on a protected ledge on the face of a cliff. Intruders are warned off with a fierce "kik-kik-kik."

Peregrine Falcon   *Falco peregrinus*

> **Field marks:** 18"; dark above; light below; **dark "mustache"**; *in flight*-medium size; lacks the dark "armpits" of the prairie falcon.
> **Status:** rare and endangered resident throughout the area and in RMNP.

The widespread use of pesticides has extirpated this species throughout much of its range. The peregrine falcon nests on cliffs, usually overlooking water, and hunts mainly birds—waterfowl, shorebirds and songbirds. Capable of "stooping" at speeds exceeding 200 miles per hour, it is our fastest bird. Specialized baffles in the nostrils allow it to breathe during the stoop. A peregrine kills its prey by overtaking it in midair and either striking it with a "fisted" foot or by grasping it with the sharp talons. Efforts are currently under-way to reintroduce it into its historic range. Peregrines have reoccupied some of their traditional eyries, or nesting sites, suggesting the efforts are at least partially successful.

American Kestrel   *Falco sparverius*

> **Field marks:** 8"; **small size; rusty back and tail** with black bars; "mustache" pointed wings; *male*-bluish wings; *female*-brown wings and tail.
> **Status:** common to abundant summer resident in the northern parts of the region; permanent resident in the sourthern parts, the lower elevations and in RMNP.

The smallest and most widespread falcon, the American kestrel feeds mostly on insects but also takes mice, frogs and small birds. It prefers open country where it hunts from its perch on a telephone wire or while hovering in the air. This kestrel nests in tree cavities, often in old woodpecker holes, in crevices in trees or cliffs or in buildings. Its warning call is "killy-killy-killy."

Prairie Falcon
J. L. Wassink

Peregrine Falcon
W. Shattil & R. Rozinski

American Kestrel female
J. L. Wassink

American Kestrel male
J. L. Wassink

49

TURKEYS, GROUSE, QUAIL, PHEASANTS, PARTRIDGE AND PTARMIGAN

TURKEYS, GROUSE, QUAIL, PHEASANTS, PARTRIDGE AND PTARMIGAN (Order Galliformes) are heavy-bodied, chicken-like land birds. Their short, heavy bills have a decurved upper mandible, ideal for foraging on seeds and insects. They rely on their powerful legs to carry them out of danger as their short, rounded wings enable them to attain full flight speed with a couple wingbeats but do not allow sustained flight. The males are more colorful than the females and often engage in elaborate courtship displays. The courting male will strut; raise or spread specialized feathers on the head, neck, or tail; inflate air sacs in the neck; beat the air with his wings or release air from specialized neck sacs to produce a variety of courtship sounds. They nest on the ground and lay large clutches (ten to fourteen) of eggs. The young hatch covered with down and leave the nest almost immediately.

Turkeys (Family Meleagrididae) are large birds with naked heads, broad wings, long legs and broad fan-shaped tails. They feed on nuts and seeds.

Wild Turkey   *Meleagris gallopavo*

Field marks: *male*–48"; *female*–36"; **large size**; dark iridescent plumage; large fan-shaped tail tipped with buff; **naked head**.
Status: local as a result of introduction.

Wild turkeys reside in the ponderosa pine forests and mixed woods along streams and rivers of the region. They move in flocks except when the hens scatter to nest in the spring. During courtship, the males spread their long, broad, colorful tails and strut and gobble—a habit that often betrays the presence of these birds even before you see them.

Grouse and Ptarmigan (Family Tetronidae) are medium-sized birds with moderate to long tails. Adapted to cold snowy climates, grouse and ptarmigan have feather-covered nostrils and feet. Lateral extensions of the scales on their toes serve as "snowshoes" in winter. Many species display elaborate courtship behavior.

Blue Grouse   *Dendragapus obscurus*

Field marks: 18"; *male*–uniform gray plumage; square, **black fan-shaped tail with gray terminal band**; *female*–brownish plumage.
Status: widespread and fairly common resident of the coniferous forests of the CR and RMNP.

The typical grouse of coniferous forests, the blue grouse, or "fool hen," is extremely tolerant of human disturbance. Early settlers are said to have killed these birds with sticks and stones. In spring, males attract the females by "hooting." The polygamous males expose a reddish patch of neck skin surrounded by a ring of white feathers. Their eyecombs act as barometers of their psychological state—yellow when calm, red when excited or disturbed. Blue grouse nest in open foothills and the broods follow ripening berry patches up the mountainside. They winter in Douglas fir thickets just below timberline, sustained by the plentiful supply of needles.

Wild Turkey Tom   J. L. Wassink

Blue Grouse   J. L. Wassink

Blue Grouse "hooting"   J. L. Wassink

Ruffed Grouse   *Bonasa umbellus*

Field marks: 17"; brown-gray plumage; black neck; **gray fan-shaped tail with black terminal band.**

Status: common resident in northwestern Wyoming and northeastern Idaho; not found farther south or in RMNP.

The most widely distributed grouse in the United States, the ruffed grouse usually inhabits aspen groves but can also be found in coniferous forests. They feed primarily on buds and catkins of aspens. In summer, insects become an important source of food. Males attract females for breeding by "drumming" from a prominent log. The sound, a muffled thumping, is produced by changes in air pressure generated by the beating wings and not by the wings striking the breast or each other as is sometimes believed.

Sharp-tailed Grouse   *Tympanuchus phasianellus*

Field marks: 18"; brown and buff plumage; **breast and sides marked with dark V's**; pointed tail.

Status: local resident in suitable habitat; not found in RMNP.

Mainly a prairie grouse, the sharptail occupies some of the more grassy habitats of the region. Before dawn on April mornings, the males gather on traditional areas called leks to dance. The dancing establishes a hierarchy among the males and determines which males do the majority of the breeding. Sharptails require native grasslands and cannot tolerate destruction of their dancing grounds. Consequently, their populations are declining because of habitat destruction.

Sage Grouse   *Centrocercus urophasianus*

Field marks: *male*–32"; *female*–21"; grayish-brown above; blackish below; long pointed tail.

Status: common in areas of sagebrush; rare resident in RMNP.

As its name implies, this grouse is restricted to sagebrush country. Unlike the other members of the order that have tough muscular gizzards to aid in digesting hard seeds and grain, sage grouse have soft membranous gizzards—indicative of their softer diet of the buds and leaves of sagebrush, supplemented with insects during the summer brood-rearing period. Like the sharptail, sage grouse gather in spring to display and "boom" on traditional leks. Sixty or more males may gather on a single lek to display. Destruction of sagebrush habitat and "booming" grounds are the main factors causing the slow but steady decline of this species.

Ruffed Grouse "drumming" T. J. Ulrich

Sharp-tailed Grouse "dancing" J. L. Wassink

Sage Grouse "booming" J. L. Wassink

53

White-tailed Ptarmigan *Lagopus leucurus*

Field marks: 13"; small; *summer*–mottled brown, black and white plumage; **white tail;** *winter*–**solid white plumage; black bill.**

Status: fairly common resident in the scattered alpine habitats of the area; common in RMNP.

The deliberate and slow-moving white-tailed ptarmigan is the only bird that spends its entire life on the alpine tundra. Its thick coat of feathers not only protects it from the elements, but also provides camouflage by matching the colors of the season. In summer, the mottled brown ptarmigan blends with its habitat. As winter approaches, the brown feathers are molted one at a time and replaced by white feathers. By the time snow arrives, the bird is pure white, except for its black eyes and beak. In spring, the process reverses, with the white feathers being replaced with brown ones until the birds once again blend with the summer landscape. Only the tail remains white all year.

The female lays her six to eight buff, faintly spotted eggs in a nest sparsely lined with grass, leaves and feathers and tucked under a small shrub or by a rock. The chicks hatch and begin searching for insects along the edges of snowfields. They also eat leaves and berries when insects are not plentiful. Even in good years, one-third of the chicks do not survive the summer.

Winter days find the white-tailed ptarmigan feeding on the leaves and buds of dwarf willow, which is the bird's main winter food. Heavily feathered feet and toes act as "snowshoes" to hold the bird up in soft snow. On winter nights, the birds burrow into the snow where they are insulated from the elements.

White-tailed Ptarmigan female, summer plumage   T. J. Ulrich

White-tailed Ptarmigan male, summer plumage   T. J. Ulrich

White-tailed Ptarmigan, eclipse plumage   W. Shattil & R. Rozinski

White-tailed Ptarmigan, winter plumage   J. L. Wassink

Pheasants, Quail and Partridge (Subfamily Phasianinae), like the rest of the family, scratch the surface of the ground for seeds and insects. In contrast to the grouse, pheasants, quail and partridge have nostrils and tarsus that are bare of feathers. In addition, these birds have bare patches of skin, instead of inflatable air sacs, for courtship displays. They use spurs on their lower legs for fighting. Neither bird featured here is native to the region or to North America, but were introduced from the Far East.

Ring-necked Pheasant   *Phasianus colchicus*

Field marks: 33"; *male*–large; **multicolored plumage**; white neck ring; **long, tapered tail**; *female*–mottled brown plumage.
Status: introduced; common near agricultural areas; not found in RMNP.

The success of the ring-necked pheasant is due in part to its widespread introduction. Hunters introduced this prized game bird to almost all available habitat. Closely linked to agriculture, pheasants feed on weed seeds, insects and waste grain. They nest in the weedy margins of agricultural cropland as well as in grain and alfalfa fields where they are often killed by mowing machines and combines. The polygamous male attracts hens in spring by beating his wings and crowing from a favored location within his home range. Although they spend summers alone or in small family groups, they often form large flocks in late winter.

Chukar   *Alectoris chukar*

Field marks: 13"; **gray back; barred black and white flanks; white face and throat; red legs.**
Status: introduced local resident in arid country; vagrant in RMNP.

Introduced from the foothills of the Himalayas, chukars found the arid country near steep rocky slopes of the region very much to their liking. They thrive in climates where summers are short and hot and winters only moderately cold and long. Snow forces them to move from the upper slopes into lower valleys, and persistently deep snow may cause heavy losses. Chukars seek bunch grass and sagebrush habitats during the spring nesting season. From mid-morning to afternoon, chukars forage for the seeds of cheatgrass, Russian thistle and other weeds. During the heat of summer, they make daily trips to water before dispersing into the brushy draws to roost for the evening.

Ring-necked Pheasant rooster J. L. Wassink

Ring-necked Pheasant hen J. L. Wassink

Chukar T. J. Ulrich

CRANES, RAILS AND COOTS (Order Gruiformes) form a diverse group of wading birds. All have long legs but other features, such as body size and shape, bill size and neck length vary considerably.

Cranes (Family Gruidae) are tall, long-legged birds with long necks and heavy bodies. Cranes fly with their head extended, distinguishing them from herons. They lay two eggs per year.

Whooping Crane   *Grus americana*

Field marks: 60" tall; white plumage; black wingtips.

Status: rare migrant in southwestern Wyoming and in the San Luis Valley; a "cross-fostered" flock at Gray's Lake NWR in eastern Idaho; not found in RMNP.

The tallest bird in North America, the extremely rare whooping crane exists in two distinct flocks. The main flock breeds in the muskeg wilderness of Wood Buffalo National Park in northwestern Canada and winters at Aransas National Wildlife Refuge on the Gulf coast of Texas. Wildlife biologists helped establish a second flock by taking eggs from the main flock to Grays Lake National Wildlife Refuge in Idaho and placing them in nests of incubating sandhill cranes. That flock has expanded but, so far, none of the birds have reproduced. In addition, there are a number of birds in captivity. The whooping crane's extremely slow reproduction rate, one per year and five years to maturity, is the main reason these birds are rare and makes rapid recovery virtually impossible.

Sandhill Crane   *Grus canadensis*

Field marks: 48" tall; gray plumage; red crown; *in flight*–**fly with neck outstretched**.

Status: local summer breeding resident in northern Colorado (North Park), in eastern Idaho (Gray's Lake), in northeastern Utah and in western Wyoming; migrant only elsewhere and in RMNP.

The stately sandhill crane mates for life and, just prior to the spring nesting, performs a remarkable ballet-like dance to reinforce that pair bond. In synchronized movement, the cranes dip, bow, leap, stretch and call to each other. As they dance, the birds use their bills to toss up sticks and grass. Sandhills nest in shallow wet meadows. They forage in wet and sometimes dry meadows for small insects, amphibians, rodents, grain, seeds and roots. After feeding in the fields all day, they invariably return to water to roost for the night. Sandhill cranes migrate in large flocks. The reddish-brown young birds mature sexually and display the slate-gray plumage of the adult when they are two years old.

Whooping Crane   T. J. Ulrich

Sandhill Crane   J. L. Wassink

Sandhill Cranes   T. J. Ulrich

59

Rails (Family Rallidae) are small to medium-sized birds that inhabit the emergent vegetation of marshes and lake shores. Their compact bodies, short necks, long legs and long toes enable them to move easily over, under and between the reeds in pursuit of the small invertebrates and insects they feed on. Shy and retiring, they are more often heard than seen. Rails build their nests just above the surface of the water and have large clutches. The adults share the domestic duties.

Virginia Rail   *Rallus limicola*

Field marks: 9"; long bill; gray cheeks; **rusty breast;** barred flanks.
Status: fairly common breeder throughout the region and in RMNP.

In spring, sounds resembling the pounding of iron on an anvil ring through the marsh. Sharp-eared birders and female Virginia rails take heed and note the presence of an amorous male Virginia rail. Almost immediately upon hatching, the chicks are ready to run, swim and dive and quickly learn to capture the snails, slugs, earthworms and insects that make up their diet.

Sora   *Porzana carolina*

Field marks: 8"; stocky body; **yellow chicken-like bill; black face and bib;** short wings; long yellowish-green legs.
Status: fairly common summer resident throughout the region and in RMNP.

Soras are seldom seen because they spend most of their time in dense stands of emergent vegetation. There, they search for insects with their heads down and their tails up and twitching almost constantly. Light enough to walk over floating water plants, they swim only when necessary. Soras place their nests in tussocks or suspend them just above the water, then lay up to eighteen eggs, arranged in two layers.

American Coot   *Fulica americana*

Field marks: 14"; **slate gray plumage;** white bill; **white under tail;** head rocks forward and backward while swimming.
Status: abundant summer resident throughout the lower elevations of the region; resident in RMNP

Look for coots on ponds or marshes with open water as well as dense stands of cattails or reeds. Highly territorial, coots sometimes battle over nesting space. Unlike the other rails, coots have lobed toes, which aid them while swimming—something they do much more than the other rails. Coots have their own peculiar way of swimming, head bobbing back and forth as they go. They may dive to depths of more than 25 feet to feed on plants or may simply steal the plants from canvasbacks or other diving ducks. Coots also eat seeds, leaves, roots, insects, snails, worms and small fish.

Virginia Rail   W. Shattil & R. Rozinski

Sora   J. L. Wassink

American Coot   J. L. Wassink

61

SHOREBIRDS, GULLS AND TERNS (Order

Charadriiformes) are small to medium-sized birds, most of whom, as their name implies, patrol the shorelines of lakes, ponds, rivers and marshes for aquatic insects and other small invertebrates. While most have long legs for feeding in up to several inches of water without getting wet, some have webbed feet that enable them to feed while swimming. A few prefer uplands to the waters edge. Long pointed wings facilitate their migratory lifestyle. This group includes the world's greatest travelers—they nest in Canada and Alaska and fly as far south as Central America to spend the winters. The sexes are similarly outfitted in rather cryptic shades of white, gray and brown.

Plovers (Family Charadriidae) are small to medium-sized shore birds with relatively short bills and shorter necks than the rest of the shorebirds. Their heads are often distinctly marked. Plovers nest directly on the ground and usually lay four eggs.

Mountain Plover   *Charadrius montanus*

Field marks: 8"; **black forecrown; white forehead**; thin black eyeline; white wing stripe.

Status: generally rare but locally fairly common breeder throughout the region; not reported in RMNP.

Although it belongs to the shorebird family, the mountain plover almost seems to avoid water. In summer, it frequents dry prairies and sagebrush country far from water, and although it moves to the Pacific Coast to spend the winter, it stays inland there too.

Killdeer   *Charadrius vociferus*

Field marks: 10"; brown back; white underneath; **double breast band**; rusty tail.

Status: widespread summer resident throughout area; resident in RMNP.

Nesting killdeer occupy a wide variety of open habitats—shorelines, pastures, golf courses, roadsides and lawns. Before and after nesting, killdeer frequent shorelines more than while nesting. Unlike some birds that will stay on the nest almost until they are stepped on, the killdeer slips off her nest while intruders are still a distance away. If the intruder continues to approach and wanders too close to the nest or the young, the adult puts on a "broken wing" act to draw the danger away from the nest. Killdeer feed mainly on insects that they pick from the surface of the ground.

Mountain Plover   W. Shattil & R. Rozinski

Killdeer   J. L. Wassink

Killdeer displaying   J. L. Wassink

63

Stilts and Avocets (Family Recurvirostridae) are medium to large shorebirds whose Latin name describes their long, thin upturned or straight bills. As their exceptionally long legs might suggest, they feed on insects and small aquatic invertebrates in deeper water than most other shorebirds.

Black-necked Stilt   *Himantopus mexicanus*

Field marks: 14"; tall slim; **black above**, white below; straight black bill; **long slender red legs**.

Status: uncommon local breeder throughout the region; not reported in RMNP.

Appropriately named, the black-necked stilt frequents the muddy or grassy shorelines of shallow fresh water, brackish or salt marshes. It walks gracefully but its legs are so long that it must bend at the knee to pick up insects from the ground. However, these stilts are no handicap when the bird feeds as it usually does—by wading through the water, daintily picking insects from the water's surface or from aquatic vegetation.

American Avocet   *Recurvirostra americana*

Field marks: 18"; **light brown head, neck and breast**; black wings with white bars; white below; **long black upturned bill**; long, thin blue-gray legs; webbed toes.

Status: fairly common summer resident in the lower elevations of the region; uncommon in RMNP.

One of the most striking shorebirds, American avocets inhabit the alkaline ponds of arid mountain basins. There, they frequent the shallows to feed on aquatic insects and other invertebrates by sweeping their bills from side to side while wading through the shallow water. The sweeping action stirs the bottom mud, exposing the small aquatic animals and insects that the bird promptly eats. Avocets nest on expansive flats, shorelines or islands with little or no vegetation, laying three or four olive blotched eggs either in a shallow depression in the sand or a small platform of grass near the water. Soon after hatching, the young leave the nest and follow the adults to the water. If the family is disturbed, the young scurry for cover while the adults use the old broken-wing ploy to distract the intruder. Avocets swim readily. Their call is a "wheet - wheet."

Black-necked Stilt   T. J. Ulrich

American Avocet   J. L. Wassink

American Avocet chick   J. L. Wassink

Sandpipers (Family Scolopacidae) are a large and diverse group of wading and upland birds clothed in dull gray, buff or brown plumage. Variations in wing, rump or tail markings identify the different species. Their legs and bills are long and slender, ideal for probing soft mud or shallow water for small invertebrates. Except for the phalaropes, the sexes are virtually identical. Sandpipers breed on the barren grounds and muskegs of the Arctic and subarctic and winter in South America.

Lesser Yellowlegs   *Tringa flavipes*

Field marks: 10"; plain gray-brown plumage; **bright yellow legs**; long, slim bill; call is a one to three note whistle; the similar greater yellowlegs is larger (14"), has a noticeably longer bill and a three to five note whistle.
Status: common migrant throughout the region; rare in RMNP.

Usually seen probing for food in the mud along the edges of marshes and slow rivers, the lesser yellowlegs is a common sight in spring. Yellowlegs also feed by skimming the invertebrates from the surface of the water or the ground. Smaller, tamer and quieter than its lookalike, the greater yellowlegs (which also migrates through the central Rockies), the lesser yellowlegs bobs its head when it is about to take flight.

Willet   *Catoptrophorus semipalmatus*

Field marks: 15"; plain, grayish-brown plumage; bluish legs; partially webbed feet; bill thicker than yellowlegs; *in flight*–**diagnostic black and white wing pattern.**
Status: migrant and/or summer resident throughout the region; rare migrant in RMNP.

Willets probe prairie marshes, seasonal ponds and ephemeral streams for mollusks, crayfish, small fish and insects. They occasionally pick invertebrates off the surface of the water. Willets nest in sloughs and along alkaline flats. Look for them in the company of avocets.

Spotted Sandpiper   *Actitus macularia*

Field marks: 8"; brown above, **spotted white below**; body usually tilted forward; **"teeters" up and down almost constantly**; flies with rapid wingbeats on down-curved wings.
Status: fairly common summer resident throughout the region and in RMNP.

Most often seen running and "teetering" along rocky or gravelly shorelines of rivers and streams, the spotted sandpiper is a solitary bird that does not flock like the other sandpipers. It is the only small sandpiper that nests throughout the central and northern United States. When disturbed, it flies out over the water on short, stiff wing beats and alights again a short distance down the shore—all the time calling "wheet-wheet-wheet." The spotted sandpiper does not probe like other sandpipers but catches insects and other invertebrates on the surface of the ground.

Lesser Yellowlegs   T. J. Ulrich

Willet   J. L. Wassink

Spotted Sandpiper   J. L. Wassink

67

Long-billed Curlew
Numenius americanus

Field marks: 24"; brown plumage; large size; **long (6"), decurved bill;** cinnamon wing linings.

Status: uncommon migrant and local summer resident in the CR; rare in RMNP.

Look for the long-billed curlew in the central Rockies during its spring migration as it feeds or rests along the shores of large lakes and reservoirs. Once it arrives on its breeding grounds, the shortgrass prairies of the Dakotas, eastern Montana and the prairie provinces of Canada, the bird nests in scattered colonies on the uplands, often far from water. The nest consists of a slight hollow in the ground lined with forbs and grasses. The sexes share incubation duties for the four eggs. While raising their young on the grasslands, curlews feed mostly on insects. However, while wintering on the tidal flats and ocean beaches of southern California and the Gulf of Mexico, they eat shellfish and other invertebrates, using their long bills like forceps to extract meals from well below the ground level. Call is a drawn out "cur-lee e e."

Marbled Godwit
Limosa fedoa

Field marks: 18"; dark, mottled above; cinnamon-buff with barring below; cinnamon wing linings; **long orange upturned bill with a black tip.**

Status: fairly common migrant throughout the region; rare migrant in RMNP.

Second in size only to the long-billed curlew, marbled godwits breed from northern Montana and North Dakota up into Canada. The female seeks out a grassy hollow on the plains in which to lay her four eggs. Marbled godwits winter along the coasts of California and the Gulf of Mexico, where, like most shorebirds, they live on a diet of insects, worms, mollusks and crustaceans. Birders will easily identify this bird by its call because it calls its own name—"god-wit". Marbled godwits often gather in small flocks and feed by rapidly thrusting their bills into the soft ground of mud flats.

Least Sandpiper
Calidris minutilla

Field marks: 6"; **sparrow size; ruddy plumage above**; short, slightly drooped black bill; olive-yellow legs and feet.

Status: common migrant throughout the region; rare in RMNP.

The least sandpiper, the smallest North American shorebird, breeds on the coastal tundra of northern Canada, and winters along the Pacific, Atlantic and Gulf coasts. The least sandpiper passes through the central Rockies in spring and fall in the company of other shorebirds. It frequents mudflats and marsh edges throughout the year, feeding in the drier mud and sand away from the edge of the water. The least sandpiper feeds either by probing in the mud or by picking food from the surface of the ground. Migrating flocks take flight as single units, zigging and zagging in unison.

Long-billed Curlew   T. J. Ulrich

Marbled Godwit   J. L. Wassink

Least Sandpiper   T. J. Ulrich

69

Long-billed Dowitcher *Limnodromus scolpaceus*

Field marks: 12"; plump profile; long, black bill; reddish below; barred flanks; *in flight*–**white rump and lower back**.
Status: fairly common migrant throughout the region; rare in RMNP.

These birds breed on northern coast of Alaska and winter on the Pacific, Atlantic, and Gulf coasts, passing through Colorado during migration in April and October. Long-billed dowitchers gather in small flocks in grassy marshes, either feeding by probing in belly-deep water or nesting on mudflats. In contrast to most shorebirds, they will often dunk their heads underwater while searching for insect larvae, tiny snails and seeds.

Common Snipe *Gallinago gallinago*

Field marks: 11"; **extremely long bill; stocky body**; short legs; brown plumage.
Status: fairly common resident throughout the region and in RMNP.

Look for the common snipe perched on a roadside fencepost near soggy meadows. Its extremely long bill makes it easy to recognize. Like the other shorebirds, the snipe uses its bill to probe for invertebrates in moist ground. When the bird detects a food item with its sensitive bill, it uses the bill's prehensile tip to quickly grasp the morsel and pull it to the surface. Snipe nest in boggy areas, often near beaver ponds, on small hummocks hidden in tall grass. The male snipe establishes his territory with "winnowing" flights—sudden, deep dives that produce a wavering sound as air rushes through the bird's outer tail feathers. When threatened, the snipe relies on its protective coloring for security, flushing only at the last instant and soon dropping back into tall vegetation.

Wilson's Phalarope *Phalaropus tricolor*

Field marks: 9"; *male*–brown plumage; white below; **dark stripe through the eye and down the neck**; long thin bill; *female*–similar to the male but with **bright chestnut markings on sides of neck and on back**.
Status: fairly common summer resident throughout lower elevations; rare in RMNP.

In this species, the females are more colorful than the males. But, the role reversal does not end with the plumage. The females also establish the territories, court the males, and, after laying the eggs, leave the small clutch for the male to incubate. Phalaropes feed both in the normal hunt-and-peck manner of the other shorebirds and by their own unique method—whirling in circles on the surface of shallow water. The spinning action creates a vortex that stirs the bottom muck and sucks it to the surface where the phalarope picks out the food without even wetting its head.

Long-billed Dowitcher VIREO/A. Morris

Common Snipe J. L. Wassink

Male Wilson's Phalarope T. J. Ulrich

71

Gulls and Terns (Family Laridae) have webbed feet, long pointed wings and are graceful and adept in flight

Gulls (subfamily Larinae) have heavy bills that hook at the tip, a feature that enables them to eat almost anything. Unlike terns, gulls often float on the water. Gulls traditionally fed on dead or dying fish or patrolled the shorelines for grasshoppers and crickets, but soon learned to take advantage of easy food provided by humans. Look for them in freshly plowed or flooded fields, city parks, sanitary landfills or even supermarket parking lots. They also sometimes act as predators by preying on the eggs and young of other birds. The sexes are similar.

Franklin's Gull *Larus pipixcan*

Field marks: 14"; dark red bill; **black head with incomplete white eye-ring**; white neck and underparts; **dark wings with white bar across wingtip.**

Status: fairly common spring migrant and abundant fall migrant throughout the area and in RMNP; local summer resident.

Franklin's gulls nest in colonies in the prairie potholes north of the central Rockies and the marshes of the Great Basin west of the central Rockies. They prefer marshes with dense stands of emergent vegetation. Unlike the other gulls in the area, which nest exclusively on land, Franklin's gulls usually build large floating nests in the reeds. These insectivores eat grasshoppers and other insects that farmers and ranchers consider pests.

Ring-billed Gull *Larus delawarensis*

Field marks: 19"; white plumage; gray wings; **black ring around bill; yellowish legs and feet.**

Status: fairly common to abundant migrant throughout the region and in RMNP; local breeder in the northern part of the region.

Like most other gulls, ring-billed gulls nest in colonies, usually on islands with little or low vegetation. These opportunistic feeders will follow a farmer's plow for overturned tidbits, frequent garbage dumps and flock to newly mown fields to eat insects. The most common gull in the region, ring-billed gulls have adapted and expanded their range—utilizing residential areas even though their traditional habitat has shrunk.

California Gull *Larus californicus*

Field marks: 19"; white plumage, dark mantle; **yellow-green legs and feet; yellow bill with red and black spots** near the tip of the lower mandible.

Status: fairly common migrant and summer resident in the CR; migrant only in RMNP.

Like ring-billed gulls, California gulls nest in colonies on sparsely vegetated islands. Opportunistic feeders, they flock anywhere food is abundant, including city parks and supermarket parking lots. In 1848, these birds descended on the swarms of crickets that were eating up the crops of the Mormon settlers, saving the crops. In return, Utah designated the California gull as the state bird. It winters along the Pacific coast of Washington, Oregon and California.

Franklin's Gull   J. L. Wassink

Ring-billed Gull   J. L. Wassink

California Gull   J. L. Wassink

Terns (subfamily Sterninae), in contrast to the heavy-bodied gulls, have thin pointed bills, narrow wings and forked tails—features that give them a more delicate and graceful appearance. They fly lightly over the water in search of small fish, plunging in a headfirst dive to capture their prey. Terns seldom alight on the water, preferring instead to rest on shore or on floating debris. They lay two or three eggs.

Caspian Tern   *Sterna caspia*

Field marks: 21"; large size; **large head**; heavy red bill; **crested black cap**; short, slightly forked tail.

Status: uncommon migrant and local breeder in Wyoming; not reported in RMNP.

The largest tern in North America, the Caspian tern is expanding its range into this area. Although it nests in large colonies elsewhere, in the central Rockies one or two pairs usually nest in a colony with another species, most often on gravel islands or beaches. This solitary bird is the least sociable of the terns and not as graceful as the smaller terns. The Caspian tern acts like a gull at times—alighting on the water and preying on the eggs and young of other birds.

Forster's Tern   *Sterna forsteri*

Field marks: 15"; pale gray above, white below; **black crown and nape**; orangish bill; **white outer edges of tail**; *similar species*–common tern has black outer edges on tail.

Status: fairly common migrant and local summer breeder in area; summer resident but no breeding confirmed in RMNP.

Forster's terns are the most common black-capped tern in the region. They prefer shallow marshes with emergent vegetation and islands for nesting. They forage over open water, plunge-diving for fish, picking bits of food from the water's surface or taking insects out of the air. They breed chiefly in the marshes of inland waters of Alberta with smaller populations breeding in California and the Great Salt Lake, and they winter in South America.

Black Tern   *Chlidonias niger*

Field marks: 10"; **black plumage**; gray wings.

Status: migrant and local summer resident throughout the region; rare migrant in RMNP.

Tame, almost friendly birds, black terns occupy marshes with abundant emergent vegetation across the interior of the continent. Nests are a shallow cup of reeds on a muskrat house or low tussock or a frail platform among the reeds. More insectivorous than the other terns, black terns may hawk insects from the air or skim them from the surface of the water.

Caspian Tern E. T. Jones

Forster's Tern J. L. Wassink
Black Tern T. J. Ulrich

PIGEONS AND DOVES (Order Columbiformes, Family

Columbidae) are ground feeding birds with small heads, short legs, long pointed wings and fan-shaped or pointed tails. They "coo" and bob their heads when they walk. Pigeons and doves eat seeds, grains, nuts and berries and need a plentiful supply of water daily, which they swallow without raising their heads as most birds must do, to help soften the dry hard seeds they eat. They lay one or two eggs (but may raise up to four broods each year) and share the incubation—the female incubates during the day and the male at night. Pigeons and doves feed their squabs (young) "pigeon milk"— a curdy mixture of skin sloughed in the crop and partially digested seeds.

Rock Dove   *Columba livia*

Field marks: 13"; large, stout body; plumage color varies widely.
Status: common resident throughout the CR; less common in higher elevations and RMNP.

This immigrant from the Old World is the wild form of the domestic pigeon. Selective and/or indiscriminate breeding of domestic stock has resulted in a wide range of colors—black, brown, white and various combinations of these colors. Rock doves usually nest in buildings or other man-made structures but also use cliffs or crevices. The nest, a loose arrangement of straw, feathers and grasses fashioned into a shallow platform, may be used to raise several broods each year.

Band-tailed Pigeon   *Columba fasciata*

Field marks: 15"; slate-blue plumage; broad, **pale terminal tail band**; **white crescent on nape**; black-tipped yellow bill.
Status: fairly common summer resident south of Wyoming-Colorado border including RMNP; rare farther north.

The largest pigeon in North America, these birds depend heavily on acorns and pine nuts for food. Band-tailed pigeons are common in oak woodlands and stands of ponderosa pine. Gregarious and somewhat nomadic, except while raising their single squab, they wander about in small flocks searching for plentiful supplies of acorns, wild fruits and berries.

Mourning Dove   *Zenaida macroura*

Field marks: 12"; small size; grayish-brown plumage; **long pointed tail**; **wings whistle in flight**.
Status: abundant breeder throughout the region and in RMNP.

The mourning dove lives and breeds in virtually all habitats in the region, making it a familiar sight to almost everyone. It nests either on the ground or in trees where it builds a haphazard pile of sticks that is easily destroyed by a stong wind. During the breeding season, the male has a small iridescent spot on his neck and his blue eye-ring and red legs intensify in color. Most mourning doves move south in fall but some winter here.

Rock Dove   J. L. Wassink

Band-tailed Pigeon   Visuals Unlimited, W. Grenfell

Mourning Dove   J. L. Wassink

OWLS (Order Strigiformes)

OWLS (Order Strigiformes) are one of the most easily recognized groups of birds. These birds of the night are equipped with large eyes set forward on their heads to provide binocular vision, which is invaluable in locating and focusing on fast-moving prey. Extremely sensitive ears, unequal in size and located behind facial discs that apparently help focus the sound, can pinpoint prey in total darkness. Flight feathers, with their soft leading edges, allow almost noiseless flight. Owls swallow small prey whole but tear larger prey into bite-sized pieces with their powerful talons and strong hooked beaks. Undigestable bones, fur and feathers are regurgitated in the form of "owl pellets." The females are generally larger than the males and begin incubating their eggs immediately after laying the first egg, allowing the young to hatch at intervals. The oldest, and therefore the largest, chick insists on being fed first. Only when he is satiated, does the next one get to eat. In lean years, the youngest and weakest may not survive, but this method maximizes the chance that at least some of the young will survive to carry on the species. Each species of owl has a distinctive call and most are easily attracted in spring by imitating or playing recordings of their calls.

Western Screech Owl   *Otus kennicottii*

Field marks: 9"; small size; **yellow eyes**; **ear tufts**; grayish plumage.
Status: fairly common breeding resident in suitable habitat throughout the area and in RMNP.

The western screech owl occupies many habitat types in the region—suburbs, orchards, farms, river bottoms, pinyon-juniper forests, aspens and ponderosa pine forests. They take mice from the meadows and large insects from the air or from foliage, as well as bats, crayfish, fish, reptiles, frogs, worms and birds wherever they can find them. Screech owls nest in tree cavities, laying four or five eggs in April. The adults defend the young fearlessly, frequently attacking trespassers who venture too near their nest.

Great Horned Owl   *Bubo virginianus*

Field marks: 22"; large size; **ear tufts**; horizontal bars on belly. *Voice –* deep, low "hoo-hoo-hoooo hoo-hoo."
Status: common breeding resident throughout the region and in RMNP.

The great horned owl is the most common owl in all types of woodlands. This highly efficient predator prefers rabbits but takes a wide variety of birds, mammals and reptiles. Remains of dogs, cats, skunks, rattlesnakes and even peregrine falcons have been found in their castings. When the February breeding season rolls around, the owls take possession of an old hawk or heron nest, a tree hollow, an appropriate ledge or crevice, or even an undisturbed corner in a building and lay two to four eggs. Like the screech owl, they are fearless when defending their young.

Young Screech Owl
J. L. Wassink

Western Screech Owl
J. L. Wassink

Young Great Horned Owl
J. L. Wassink

Great Horned Owl
J. L. Wassink

Long-eared Owl

Asio otus

Field marks: 15"; medium size; **long ear tufts;** smaller, slimmer than great horned owl; **vertical barring on belly.**

Status: uncommon resident throughout much of the region and in RMNP.

Like the great horned owl, the long-eared owl frequents a wide variety of habitats, although it seems to prefer dense forests or streamside timber. The highly nocturnal long-eared owl hunts small mammals, mostly mice, by night and finds an inconspicuous spot close to the trunk of a shady tree to roost during the day. Like many other owls, it remodels an old crow, hawk, heron or magpie nest to suit its needs and lays from three to seven white eggs. Its buoyant and erratic flight is easily recognized.

Short-eared Owl

Asio flammeus

Field marks: 15"; medium size; "earless"; **light belly with vertical streaks;** *in flight*–black wrist-marks; flies with a buoyant lilt.

Status: uncommon resident throughout most of the region; not found in RMNP.

An owl of open country, the short-eared owl commonly perches on fence posts or drifts low over the grasslands, searching for prey. This diurnal owl often hunts rodents in broad daylight. Since it inhabits areas without trees, it sleeps and nests on the ground. Powered by slow relaxed wing strokes, its flight has an erratic bouncing character.

Great Gray Owl

Strix nebulosa

Field marks: 28"; large size; large head; **no ear tufts; concentric circles in facial discs;** yellow eyes; **white "bow tie."**

Status: rare resident of montane forests in Wind River Mountains of western Wyoming and in extreme eastern Idaho; then north along the Continental Divide.

An inhabitant of open meadows and forest clearings near mature stands of conifers, the great gray owl hunts from an elevated perch. It takes hares, pine squirrels, mice and small birds, but its main prey is pocket gophers. Although seldom seen, the great gray owl is tame and almost indifferent to people. It confiscates an old hawk or crow nest to contain its two to five eggs, which it lays when there is still snow on the ground. Less nocturnal than some owls, the great gray often hunts at dawn and dusk. This owl of the north sports a thick coat of feathers that make it look larger than it really is.

Long-eared Owl

Short-eared Owl

Great Gray Owl

Great Gray Owl

Northern Pygmy Owl

Glaucidium gnoma

Field marks: 7"; small size; **long tail**; no ear tufts; false eyes in back of head; black streaked flanks.

Status: uncommon resident in northwestern Wyoming, eastern Idaho and central Colorado; rare in RMNP.

The northern pygmy owl inhabits montane forests, sometimes to elevations as high as 12,000 feet in Colorado. More diurnal than the other small owls, it often hunts during the day. From its perch on an exposed branch or the top of a tall shrub, the pygmy owl scouts for insects, lizards, birds and small mammals, taking more birds than most other owls. Woodpecker holes or similar cavities provide shelter for its three or four white eggs and, later, its young.

Burrowing Owl

Athene cunicularia

Field marks: 9"; small size; **long, nearly bare legs**; no ear tufts; has habit of "bowing"; nests in burrows.

Status: local, summer resident in plains of the region; rare in RMNP.

Most owls nest in trees; burrowing owls, as their name suggests, nest in burrows in the ground, usually located in abandoned prairie dog burrow or a burrow confiscated from another rodent. The owls modify the tunnel and nesting chamber each year by vigorously digging and scratching with their feet, beak and wings. The adults often decorate the nest with bits of paper and chunks of dry manure. Because of their dependence on abandoned burrows for nesting, the numbers of burrowing owls have declined along with the prairie dog populations. Burrowing owls are largely diurnal and feed on insects, small reptiles and small mammals. When disturbed, they bob and bow before either flying away a short distance or scurrying into their burrows. When prey is plentiful, they may raise from five to seven youngsters each year.

Northern Saw-whet Owl

Aegolius acadicus

Field marks: 8"; small size; **black bill**; **reddish-brown color**; facial disc lacks black border. *Similar species* –boreal owl has **black border** on facial discs, and a yellowish bill.

Status: year-round residents in montane forests of the region as well as in RMNP.

This small earless owl takes shelter in old woodpecker holes in a variety of woodlands, from river bottoms to coniferous forests. The saw-whet lays five or six eggs in the cavity and, when the young hatch, the adults feed them any prey of appropriate size—usually insects and mice but also rats and squirrels. Saw-whets stay at home for most of the year but, in a harsh winter, they may move to lower elevations in search of easier hunting. The boreal owl, which inhabits higher elevations in the region, closely resembles the saw-whet in both appearance and habits. Both owls tolerate human disturbance and can usually be approached quite closely while roosting.

Northern Pygmy Owl
J. L. Wassink

Burrowing Owls
J. L. Wassink

Burrowing Owl
J. L. Wassink

Northern Saw-whet Owl
W. Shattil & R. Rozinski

NIGHTJARS (Order Caprimulgiformes, Family Caprimulgidae) feed
in flight by scooping insects out of midair. Huge scoop-like mouths surrounded by long whiskers help funnel insects into their mouths. Short, weak legs barely allow them to waddle around on the ground. They occasionally perch in trees but, when they do so, they perch lengthwise on the branches rather than crosswise like most birds.

Common Nighthawk   *Chordeiles minor*

> **Field marks:** 8"; mottled brown and gray plumage; tiny beak; long pointed wings; **white bar on lower wing**; square or slightly notched tail.
>
> **Status:** fairly common summer resident in the region and in RMNP at elevations below 7,500 feet.

Look for common nighthawks in the early evening, flying about erratically in pursuit of insects. Their bat-like feeding behavior has earned them the nickname "bull-bat." During the day, they sometimes perch on fence posts, on low rocks or on the ground. Common nighthawks feed exclusively on flying insects, which they scoop out of the air with their cavernous mouths. The birds arrive in Colorado in late May and lay their two eggs sometime in June. They build no nest, laying the eggs on the bare ground in an exposed location. In cities, nighthawks often nest on rooftops, especially those with graveled surfaces.

SWIFTS AND HUMMINGBIRDS (Order Apodiformes).
Apodiformes literally means "without feet." The members of this order do have feet, albeit tiny and weak, but they are masters of flight.

Swifts (Family Apodidae) are built for speed with torpedo-shaped bodies and flat, narrow, swept-back wings. In flight, they resemble swallows, but the swift's wings beat in a more hurried tempo. Creatures of the air, they eat, drink and even breed on the wing.

Black Swift   *Cypseloides niger*

> **Field marks:** 7"; **uniform dark color**; slightly forked tail; large size.
>
> **Status:** local summer resident in region, breeder in RMNP.

The largest American swift, the black swift nests in steep, narrow canyons, usually near waterfalls. The females lay a single egg as late as July and both adults feed the young a diet of regurgitated insects, mostly flying ants. During periods of cool, rainy weather, when flying insects are scarce, the adults may leave for several days to search for areas with more plentiful insects. The young, left to themselves, go into a torpor until the adults return to feed them again. Although they can survive up to ten days without food, the young grow and mature faster in warm years when they are fed regularly. Due to its small numbers and inaccessible habitat, little is known about the biology of the black swift. The white-throated swift (*Aeronautes sacxatalis*) replaces the black swift in arid country and is much more common in this region.

84

Common Nighthawk J. L. Wassink

Nighthawk with twelve-day-old chicks J. L. Wassink

Black Swift T. J. Ulrich

Hummingbirds (Family Trochilidae) are the smallest North American birds and put out the greatest output of energy per unit of weight of any known animal except insects in flight. To keep up with those energy demands, hummers sip nectar from flowers for calories and eat small insects and spiders for protein. With their long, thin bills and tube-like tongues they reach deep into tubular flowers to obtain nectar. To move efficiently from flower to flower requires remarkable powers of flight and hummers can do it all—fly forward, fly backward, fly straight up, fly straight down, hover, pivot and even perform backwards somersaults. Among the most brightly colored of the birds, they wear dazzling iridescent colors on their backs and the males sport distinctive brightly-colored, iridescent throat patches called gorgets.

Black-chinned Hummingbird   *Archilochus alexandri*

Field marks: 3½"; *male*–**black gorget** with purplish border and a white band; *female*–green above; white below; small white spot behind eye.

Status: fairly common summer resident in the western part of the region; not usually found in RMNP.

This bird usually inhabits streamside habitats in dry regions but can also occupy oak/juniper/aspen habitats with abundant flowers. The black-chinned hummer also captures insects like a flycatcher by hawking them from a conspicuous perch. Like most hummingbirds, they build tiny cup-shaped nests of tiny plant parts held together by cobwebs. They lay two bean-sized eggs that hatch about twenty days later. The mother thrusts her long bill down the her youngster's throats and feeds them by regurgitation. The young fledge in about three weeks and are on their own in about five weeks. Courtship flight traces a deep U-shaped figure in the sky.

Rufous Hummingbird   *Selasphorous rufus*

Field marks: 3¾"; *male*–**scarlet gorget; rusty back; orange-red sides**; *female*–green above; **rust color in center of rump**; white below.

Status: summer resident in northwestern Wyoming; fairly common migrant throughout the rest of the region and in RMNP.

Ranging as far north as Alaska, the rufous is the most northerly of the hummingbirds. Very aggressive defenders of feeding and nesting territories, they may attempt to drive away blackbirds and chipmunks as well as other hummingbirds. In normal flight, their wingbeats create a subdued hum, and in a rapid dive, they produce a loud whine. Rufous hummingbirds, as well as other hummingbirds, become torpid at night. Torpidity is a state in which the body temperature drops almost to that of the surrounding air and both the heart rate and respiration rate decrease dramatically. When nighttime temperatures drop below 60 degrees, the birds may save as much as 98 percent of the energy it would take for them to maintain their normal body temperature. Courtship flight traces an upright oval in the air.

Male Black-chinned Hummingbird
T. J. Ulrich

Male Rufous Hummingbird
J. L. Wassink

Female Rufous Hummingbird, wings upside-down on backstroke J. L. Wassink

87

Calliope Hummingbird   *Stellula calliope*

Field marks: 2¾"; *male*–**striped scarlet gorget**; greenish back; small size; *female*–green back; white underparts; short tail; no rust in center of rump.

Status: common summer resident in northern and western Wyoming, eastern Idaho and northwestern Utah; migrant only in Colorado and in RMNP.

The scientific name of this bird means, loosely, "beautiful little star" in reference to its small size and brilliant colors. The smallest bird in North America, the calliope hummingbird is also the second most northerly hummer, behind the rufous. It inhabits the borders of mountain meadows surrounded by coniferous forests as well as alpine areas as high as 11,000 feet. The tiny nest, camouflaged with lichens on the outside, lies under an overhanging branch in a conifer, well hidden and protected from the elements. The calliope's pendulum-like courtship flight traces a shallow U.

Broad-tailed Hummingbird   *Selasphorous platycercus*

Field marks: 3¾"; *male*–**solid scarlet gorget; green back; loud buzzing flight**; *female*–green back; pale gray underparts; **rufous on flanks and outer tail feathers**.

Status: common summer resident throughout most of the region and the most common hummingbird in RMNP.

The common nesting hummingbird of the region, the broad-tailed hummingbird lives at forest edges at elevations up to 11,000 feet. As with the other hummers as well, the males arrive on the breeding grounds first, usually around mid-May in the RMNP area. There, the male launches his J-shaped courtship flight from deciduous bushes, such as streamside willow thickets. Unable to resist this dazzling display, the female chooses a nesting site nearby, often on a small limb suspended over a bubbling stream. The two outer primaries of the broad-tailed hummingbird's wings narrow at the tips, forming slots. During flight, air rushes through those slots producing a unique trilling sound. Distinguish the broad-tailed hummingbird's "rattling" sound from the more "buzz-like" sound of the rufous hummingbird in flight.

Male Calliope Hummingbird   J. L. Wassink

Female Broad-tailed Hummingbird   W. Shattil & R. Rozinski
Male Broad-tailed Hummingbird   W. Shattil & R. Rozinski

KINGFISHERS (Order Coraciiformes, Family Alcedinidae), as their
name implies, live primarily on fish. These chunky, compact birds have
large bills, large heads accentuated by a ragged erectile crest, tiny feet, short
tails and short, rounded wings. They are solitary except while nesting.

Belted Kingfisher   *Ceryle alcyon*

Field marks: 13"; **oversized blue head**; white neck; blue back; **large
heavy bill; big unruly crest**; bluish breast band; *female*-similar but with
an **additional chestnut breast band**.

Status: fairly common summer resident throughout the region and in
RMNP.

Belted kingfishers perch on a branch or stump near or over water
containing an abundance of small fish. From here they dive headlong into
the water in pursuit of fish, amphibians, crustaceans and aquatic insects.
After the speed of the dive carries them completely underwater, they
emerge, carrying some small hapless creature in their bill. Kingfishers nest
in burrows in cutbanks, usually along streams but also along roads, borrow
pits, or other similar vertical banks. They dig the burrows with their bills,
pushing the dirt out with their small feet. The female may lay as many as
eight eggs, which the pair incubates in shifts. Once the youngsters hatch,
their voracious appetites keep both adults busy bringing food.

WOODPECKERS (Order Piciformes, Family Picidae) have heavy
skulls and thick, heavy chisel-like bills that enable them to reach the wood-
boring insects and larvae hidden under the bark or in rotting wood. Strong
feet and claws and stiff tail feathers help them hold on to vertical surfaces
and brace their bodies in position while hammering. Thus equipped, most
of them forage on the trunks and large branches of trees. Some members also
take insects from the bark, the air, the foliage or the ground and also eat
nuts, berries and fruit. In spring, woodpeckers "drum" to attract mates and
establish their territories.

Northern Flicker   *Colaptes auratus*

Field marks: 12"; gray head and neck with tan forehead; **grayish-brown
back and belly** with black breast patch; **red or yellow flash** on underside
of wings in flight; white rump; *male*-has red or black mustache.

Status: common resident throughout the region and in RMNP.

Flickers reside virtually anywhere there are trees, but they prefer open
woodlands to dense forests. Flickers feed mostly on ants and other insects
that they find by probing the ground rather than chipping out of wood. They
also eat berries. Nesting cavities in trees, utility poles and sometimes in the
sides of buildings protect the six to eight eggs. Abandoned flicker holes
provide nesting sites for cavity nesters such as owls, buffleheads, kestrels,
and starlings that are unable to excavate their own cavities.

Belted Kingfisher　　　E. T. Jones

Male Northern Flicker　　　**Female Northern Flicker**
J. L. Wassink　　　J. L. Wassink

Lewis' Woodpecker

Melanerpes lewis

Field marks: 11"; grayish-black back; **rose-red breast and belly; dark red face**.

Status: local summer resident in forested areas of the lower elevations; migrant in RMNP.

The Lewis woodpecker's feeding habits are unique among woodpeckers—it catches insects on the wing, sometimes hawking them from the air like a flycatcher. It also feeds on fruits and nuts when those foods are available. When moving through its habitat of very open pine forests, the Lewis woodpecker often perches on fenceposts or stumps rather than clinging to the sides of the perch like most other woodpeckers. It nests in dead trees or in abandoned cavities drilled by other woodpeckers.

Yellow-bellied Sapsucker

Sphyrapicus varius

Field marks: 8"; *male*-black above; light below; **patches of red on crown, nape and throat**; *female*-lacks red on nape and throat.

Status: common summer resident throughout most of the region and in RMNP.

These birds frequent all types of woodlands but seem to prefer spruce and aspen groves, which provide the birds with both food and shelter. Sapsuckers drill a parallel series of holes in the bark of aspens. The holes, drilled at a slightly downward angle, create tiny reservoirs of sap on which the sapsucker feeds. They also feed on the insects that are attracted by the flowing sap. The cambium layer of inner bark provides another primary item in their diet. Sapsuckers excavate nest holes in live aspens to house their four to six white eggs and young.

Williamson's Sapsucker

Sphyrapicus thyroideus

Field marks: 8"; dark plumage; **black breastband; no red on head or nape**.

Status: common summer resident in northwestern Wyoming and eastern Idaho and south from northern Colorado and eastern Utah; common in RMNP.

These timid birds nest in mature stands of Douglas fir, aspen, lodgepole pine or even in open meadows. Williamson's sapsuckers occupy similar habitat to yellow-bellied sapsuckers, but tend toward higher elevations (between 6,500 and 8,500 feet in Colorado). They usually nest in dead aspens or fir trees but also use pines for both nesting and feeding. Williamson's sapsuckers eat sap and insects, probing for bugs in the bark and nabbing them from the air.

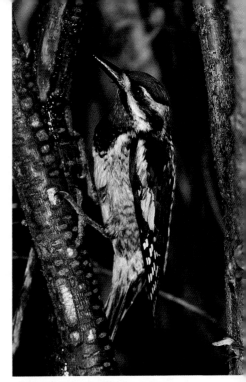

Lewis Woodpecker
T. J. Ulrich

**Male Yellow-bellied
(Red-naped) Sapsucker** L. Kaiser

**Female Yellow-bellied
Sapsucker** E. T. Jones

Williamson's Sapsucker
W. Shattil & R. Rozinski

Downy Woodpecker *Picoides pubescens*

Field marks: 6"; black and white plumage; **white underparts**; white back; black wings barred with white; **bill half the length of the head; outer tail feathers with two or more black bars**; *male*-red patch on nape.
Status: common resident throughout the region and in RMNP.

One of the most common and widespread woodpeckers in North America, the downy uses all types of wooded habitat. The downy woodpecker forages for insects on the small upper and outer branches and twigs. Watch this bird as it taps on the branch, moves on, taps again, and finally chips away at the wood when it detects a likely insect tunnel. Once it breaches the tunnel, the bird snakes its long barbed tongue down the hole, entangles the insect or grub, then withdraws and eats it. In summer, when insects are plentiful, the downy takes bugs from the surface of the branches and from the foliage. In winter, when times are tougher, they spend much more time chipping for their meals. They are regular visitors at suet feeders provided by kind-hearted bird watchers. The downy shares its habitat with the very similar but larger and more powerful hairy woodpecker. The hairy woodpecker tends to forage more on the larger branches.

Hairy Woodpecker *Picoides villosus*

Field marks: 8"; black and white plumgae; white back; black wings barred with white; **bill longer than half the length of head; white outer tail feathers usually not marked**; *male*-red patch on nape.
Status: common resident throughout the region and in RMNP.

The hairy woodpecker requires habitat similar to the downy's, but, unlike the downy, does not frequent woodlots. The hairy woodpecker feeds on the larvae of wood-boring beetles, particularly the western pine bark beetle. It feeds more on the trunk and larger vertical branches of the trees than the downy. The hairy woodpecker is also shyer than the downy and usually flies ahead of an intruder rather than simply moving upward in the tree as the downy often does.

Three-toed Woodpecker *Picoides tridactylus*

Field marks: 9"; **barred, ladder-like**, black and white pattern on back and flanks; *male*-yellow crown; **three toes** (most woodpeckers have four toes).
Status: local resident in region and in RMNP.

Three-toed woodpeckers claim their territory in newly and severely burned-over forests. Almost immediately after a fire, these birds move into the area. They chip off flakes of bark to expose bark-boring beetles that infest the recently killed trees. Three-toed woodpeckers drill cavities for their nests in a dead spruce or fir and raise four or five young. After four or five years, the birds move on, leaving the holes for bluebirds, nuthatches and other cavity-nesting birds incapable of drilling their own cavities.

Male Downy Woodpecker
J. L. Wassink

Female Downy Woodpecker
J. L. Wassink

Male Hairy Woodpecker
T. J. Ulrich

Three-toed Woodpecker
T. J. Ulrich

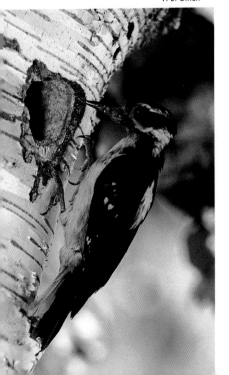

95

PERCHING BIRDS (Order Passeriformes) include almost three-fifths of all living birds. Both size extremes, the two-foot-long raven and the four- to six-inch kinglets, live in this region. Some of the most adaptive and intelligent members of the bird world are passerines. The common feature among the perching birds is feet with four highly moveable toes, three toes pointing forward and one backward, that are ideally suited to gripping a twig, branch, wire, reed or grass stem. Muscles and tendons automatically tighten their grip if the bird begins to fall backward.

Tyrant-Flycatchers (Family Tyrannidae) includes the flycatchers, pewees, phoebes and kingbirds. The family is named for their habit of catching flying insects on the wing. They sit quietly on a perch, then suddenly dart into the air to snap up insects, often with an audible click of the bill. These "tyrants" fiercely defend their nesting territories. Most species are neutral shades of gray, brown, olive-green and yellow. Although often best distinquished by voice, the presence or absence of an eye-ring and wing bars and the color of the bill will help you identify the different species.

Eastern Kingbird *Tyrannus tyrannus*

Field marks: 9"; slate-gray head and upperparts; **white underparts**; broad fan-shaped tail tipped with broad white band.
Status: common summer resident throughout the region and in RMNP.

As it flies with short, quick wingbeats, the eastern kingbird's wings seem to quiver. Conspicuous, noisy and aggressive, a kingbird will fearlessly attack a hawk, crow or any other bird that enters its territory. It frequents open country with scattered trees—often near water. There, it waits on an exposed perch, occasionally flying out to snap up an insect. In addition to the more than 200 species of insects it eats, the eastern kingbird dines on the fruits and seeds of more than 40 different plant species.

Western Kingbird *Tyrannus verticalis*

Field marks: 9"; pale gray head and upper parts; white throat; **pale yellow underparts**; white edges on tail.
Status: common summer resident throughout the region and in RMNP.

This kingbird frequents open country with occasional trees and shrubs. There, it darts out from a conspicuous perch in a tree, low bush, fence or tall weed to catch and eat insects. The western kingbird is not as aggressive as its eastern cousin, sometimes even sharing its nesting tree with others of its kind. Western kingbirds usually nest in a tree but also use bushes, utility poles, water towers, electrical substations, windmills and many other unusual locations.

Eastern Kingbird
J. L. Wassink

Western Kingbird
W. Shattil & R. Rozinski

Eastern Kingbird   J. L. Wassink

Say's Phoebe
Sayornis saya

Field marks: 8"; **rusty brown on lower breast and belly**; frequently twitches tail downward when perched.

Status: fairly common summer resident throughout the lower elevations of the region; migrant in RMNP.

A typical flycatcher, Say's phoebe snatches its insect meals from the air. It is found in arid country, usually away from water—dry sagebrush and grassland prairies and sunny canyons. It lives in agricultural areas nesting around ranch buildings, in niches in rock walls and on cut banks—anywhere with a firm shelf to support the nest. Built without mud, the nest is a flat structure of grasses and lined with wool and hair.

Willow Flycatcher
Empidonax traillii

Field marks: 6"; brownish-green back, whitish underparts; faint eye-ring; orange lower mandible; song of the willow flycatcher is a dry **"FITZ-bew"** while that of the virtually identical alder flycatcher is " fee-BEE-o."

Status: common summer resident throughout the region and in RMNP.

The willow flycatcher occupies a wide variety of habitats—from brushy fields to willow thickets, from weedlots to open woodlands. It catches most insects in flight. The willow flycatcher places its well-hidden nest low in a tree or bush. Although easy to recognize as one of the *Empidonax* species of flycatchers, it is difficult to identify the species. In fact, experts generally agree that there are often greater individual plumage differences between individuals within a species than there are between species. All the *Empidonax* flycatchers look very much like the bird in the photograph and their songs provide the best way to diiferentiate them in the field. The willow flycatcher can be positively identified by its "FITZ-bew" call, which emphasizes the first syllable. The call of the alder flycatcher has its emphasis on the second syllable.

Western Wood-pewee
Contopus sordidulus

Field marks: 8"; dusky gray-brown plumage; **two whitish wing bars; no eye-ring**; dull dark-colored bill; voice is a nasal descending "pheer."

Status: common summer resident throughout the region.

The western wood-pewee often seen perches on a dead branch at the edge of a forest clearing. It periodically flits out to snatch a bee, wasp, ant, fly or other insect from the air with an audible snap of its bill. This bird beautifully crafts its nest, camouflaging it with lichens, in a crotch on a horizontal branch from 15 to 25 feet above the ground.

Say's Phoebe W. Shattil & R. Rozinski

Willow Flycatcher J. L. Wassink

Western Wood-pewee J. L. Wassink

99

Swallows (Family Hirundinidae) are small, fast-flying, streamlined birds that catch and eat insects on the wing. On long, pointed wings swallows swoop and glide in pursuit of insects, often skimming just over the surface of water, occasionally dipping down to pick a bug off the surface or to take a sip of water. Their wide mouth gape is useful in the final capture. On short legs and tiny feet they perch on wires and thin branches but seldom walk. Swallows tolerate humans and often nest in buildings or bird houses. In fall, they gather in great flocks to feed, roost and migrate.

Barn Swallow   *Hirundo rustica*

Field marks: 7"; *male*-metallic blue-black above; red-brown forehead and breast; deeply forked tail; *female*-similar but with slightly duller colors.

Status: common summer resident throughout the area and in RMNP.

Swift and graceful, barn swallows are, without a doubt, one of the most familiar and best loved birds in America. They gather in groups at mud puddles or on muddy shorelines to collect the material to construct their cup-shaped mud nests. Formerly limited by a shortage of suitable cliffs on which to build their nests, these birds have become much more wide ranging with the spread of civilization and the accompanying proliferation of barns and other buildings on which to nest. Look for barn swallows perching on utility lines or swooping back and forth overhead in pursuit of insects.The closest these birds come to singing is a musical twittering that they usually utter while in flight. Barn swallows breed from April to June and fly south in September or early October.

Cliff Swallow   *Hirundo pyrrhonota*

Field marks: 6"; black crown, back, wings and tail; dark rufous throat, neck and rump; pale forehead; dark square-tipped tail.

Status: abundant summer resident throughout the region and in RMNP.

Cliff swallows locate their mud nests on the outside of bridges, barns, hotels, observation towers and other buildings as well as the traditional cliffs. They build their bulbous nests in colonies, often stacked on top of one another. The side entrance holes usually face downward. Cliff swallows can be seen in the central Rockies from April to September.

Barn Swallow   J. L. Wassink

Barn Swallow at nest   J. L. Wassink

Cliff Swallow at nest   J. L. Wassink

Violet-green Swallow   *Tachycineta thalassina*

Field marks: 5½"; **dark above with a green or purplish sheen**; white below; white patches on side of rump almost meet over the tail; **white on sides of neck extends up on neck and over eyes.**

Status: common to abundant summer resident throughout the region and in RMNP.

Found only in the western United States, violet-green swallows are birds of forests and steep-walled canyons. There, they seek out a suitable tree cavity, line it with straw and feathers and lay their four to seven eggs. Violet-greens forage at greater heights than the other swallows. They nest in June or July and fly south again in late August to spend the cold months along the coast of southern California and Mexico.

Tree Swallow   *Tachycineta bicolor*

Field marks: 6"; *male*-**steely blue-black** or green above; white below; triangular shaped wings; square tail; *female*-similar but with slightly duller colors.

Status: common to abundant summer resident throughout the region and in RMNP.

Tree swallows are the first swallows to arrive in the spring and the last to head south in the fall. They prefer more open country, often near water, than their smaller cousin, the violet-green swallow. Like the violet-green, they are cavity nesters, often nesting in aspens. Tree swallows compete with mountain bluebirds, common flickers and house wrens for the available cavities. The only swallows to winter regularly in the United States, tree swallows may winter in Florida, along the Gulf of Mexico, and in central and southern California (along the Salton Sea and the Colorado River).

Bank Swallow   *Riparia riparia*

Field marks: 5"; smallest of the North American swallows; **brown back**; white underparts; **brown breast band**; slightly forked tail; *similar species*-rough-winged swallow lacks breast band.

Status: fairly common summer resident throughout the region and in RMNP.

Widespread across the United States except in the south, these compact swallows nest in colonies in the vertical cuts of riverbanks, gravel pits or roadsides. Using only their thin, weak feet and tiny bills, they dig a three-foot tunnel into the bank, at a slightly upward angle to prevent flooding, and lay their four to seven eggs. The similar rough-winged swallow, which also lives throughout the central Rockies, utilizes similar locations but nests individually rather than in colonies. In flight, the slightly larger rough-winged swallow has a slower and more fluid tempo to its wingbeats while those of the bank swallow are shallow and rapid.

Violet-green Swallow   J. L. Wassink

Tree Swallow   J. L. Wassink

Bank Swallow   J. L. Wassink

103

Jays (Family Corvidae) are among the best known of the birds. Large (10 to 25 inches) and conspicuous (black, blue, gray, green or black and white), intelligent and boisterous, these raucous birds adapt extremely well to changing conditions. As a result, they thrive in spite of drastic changes in their environment and persecution by humans. Jays are sturdy birds with stout, pointed bills. They eat almost anything—animal or vegetable. The sexes are similar and the nests are bulky structures of twigs and branches. Some species migrate while others do not. Most are gregarious.

Black-billed Magpie   *Pica pica*

Field marks: 20"; looks **black and white** from a distance and in poor light, shines green-blue metallic when close up; **long tail**.
Status: common to abundant resident throughout the CR and in RMNP.

An inhabitant of open country, the magpie is common and highly visible in the sagebrush-grassland habitats of the lower elevations. It is bold, inquisitive and always suspicious. Its loud "mahg" call is easy to recognize. The magpie builds its nest—a large, dome-shaped mass of sticks with a side entrance—in a thorny shrub or tree. Owls and other birds and mammals often take over the nests after the magpies have deserted them. Magpies walk or hop when on the ground and feed on virtually anything that is vegetable or animal.

American Crow   *Corvus brachyrhynchos*

Field marks: 20"; **jet black plumage**; **stout bill**; call is **"caw, caw, caw."**
Status: fairly common resident throughout the region and in RMNP.

American crows usually inhabit farm country with a mix of cultivated fields, pastures, scattered woodlots and fence rows. There, they eat displaced grasshoppers and mice in newly mown hayfields, waste grain in harvested grain fields, and choice tidbits in area landfills. Although wary of humans, crows are taking up residence in cities and towns. With their nests in the forks of trees high above the ground, they are undisturbed and yet have access to the food sources provided by humans.

Common Raven   *Corvus corax*

Field marks: 24"; **solid black plumage** but bigger and heavier than the crow; longer wings, wedge-shaped tail; **call is a "croa-a-ak."**
Status: fairly common resident throughout the region and in RMNP.

Common ravens prefer the coniferous forests of the mountains to the farmlands of the flats. Ravens share the usual opportunistic feeding habits of the other jays, but also act like raptors and consume rodents, rabbits, nestling birds, bird eggs, moles and frogs. They are excellent fliers and often perform acrobatic feats and spectacular dives during courtship. Ravens build bulky stick nests on ledges in open terrain or in steep-walled canyons.

Black-billed Magpie J. L. Wassink

American Crow J. L. Wassink

Common Raven T. J. Ulrich

105

Gray Jay   *Perisoreus canadensis*

Field marks: 12"; *adult*-**gray plumage; short bill**; white forehead; black nape; *juvenile*-sooty black.

Status: fairly common resident of the higher elevation forests throughout the area and in RMNP.

Also called "Canada jays," these residents of lodgepole pine and spruce forests feed on fruits, berries, insects and carrion. Tame and unafraid, they have earned their nickname "camp robbers" by such brazen acts as stealing bread from plates and even bacon from the frying pan. Gray jays have loose, fluffy plumage that allows almost noiseless flight. Early in the year, when the snow is still on the ground and the temperatures are low, they build their bulky nest in a hidden spot in a pine or spruce tree.

Steller's Jay   *Cyanocitta stelleri*

Field marks: 13"; **dark blue with sooty black head and neck**.

Status: fairly common to common resident of the coniferous forests in the region and in RMNP.

The western equivalent of the eastern blue jay, the Steller's jay is noisy and boisterous. It inhabits most of the coniferous forests of the Rocky Mountains but is characteristic of the yellow pines. The Steller's jay begins nesting in May and the young hatch in June. Opportunistic like the other jays, it feeds on seeds, berries, insects and even the eggs and young of other birds. It's call is a raucous "shack-shack-shack."

Pinyon Jay   *Gymnorhinus cyanocephalus*

Field marks: 11"; **light blue plumage**; short tail; long bill.

Status: fairly common resident of the lower elevations in the region and in RMNP.

Closely tied to the pinyon-juniper belt of the western states, pinyon jays survive mostly on pinyon nuts. Crow-like in some of their behavior, they walk rather than hop when on the ground. Pinyon jays nest in colonies and help each other feed and raise their young. In winter, they wander erratically in huge flocks in search of sufficient food.

Clark's Nutcracker   *Nucifraga columbiana*

Field marks: 13"; gray plumage; **long bill; black and white wings**; short tail; long sharply pointed bill; **flashy white wing and tail patches visible in flight**.

Status: common residents throughout the region and in RMNP.

Look for Clark's nutcrackers near extensive stands of conifers, often near timberline, where they use their long bills to extract the seeds from the treetop cones. They also gather grubs from the bark, insects from the air and scraps from picnickers. Nutcrackers, like some of the other jays, often store food in caches, finding these stored tidbits even under two feet of snow.

Gray Jay   J. L. Wassink

Steller's Jay   J. L. Wassink

Pinyon Jay   T. J. Ulrich

Clark's Nutcracker   J. L. Wassink

107

Titmice and Chickadees (Family Paridae), spritely little birds, commonly visit bird feeders. Tame, cheery and friendly, they flit to and fro after seeds that they wedge in crevices and hammer open with their bill. In winter, they feed on dormant insects and spider eggs that they glean from the twigs and bark of trees and bushes. Although they are cavity nesters, they cannot excavate a hollow unless the wood is well-rotted. Consequently, they often finish work on holes begun but abandoned by woodpeckers.

Black-capped Chickadee　　　　　*Parus atricapillus*

Field marks: 5¾"; small size; gray and white plumage; **black cap and bib**; white cheeks; buffy flanks; **"chick-a-dee-dee-dee" call is diagnostic.**
Status: common resident throughout the region and in RMNP.

Black-capped chickadees prefer hardwood forests and woodlots in the valleys, occupying slightly lower elevations than the similar mountain chickadees. When they venture up the mountain slopes, they frequent aspen groves and deciduous forests. In winter, they are easily attracted to feeders by suet and sunflower seeds. Although they do not accept bird houses as readily as wrens or bluebirds, they do use them occasionally so it may be worth the effort to put up a house for these spritely little birds.

Mountain Chickadee　　　　　*Parus gambeli*

Field marks: 6"; small size; gray and white plumage; black cap and bib; **white eyebrow**; white cheeks.
Status: common in the higher elevations of the region and in RMNP.

Although their ranges overlap to some degree, mountain chickadees prefer coniferous woods at slightly higher elevations than the similar black-capped chickadees. They build their nests in rotting stumps or snags and raise two and sometimes three broods with as many as nine youngsters in each brood. Steadily uttering their hoarse "chick-a-dee," they search twigs, foliage and bark for caterpillars, plant lice and insect eggs.

Plain Titmouse　　　　　*Parus inornatus*

Field marks: 5½"; uniform gray plumage; **erect crest**.
Status: fairly common resident in Utah and Colorado and north to the southwestern corner of Wyoming; not found in RMNP.

The smallest crested birds in the region, plain titmice are not sociable like the other members of the family. Slower and less agile than the chickadees, they usually reside in open mixed woodlands of oak and pinyon-juniper. There, they cling to the undersides of boughs as they search for insects. They also eat seeds and fruit when available. Cavities in rotten stumps or branch stubs provide shelter for their nests.

Black-capped Chickadee   J. L. Wassink

Mountain Chickadee   J. L. Wassink

Plain Titmouse   T. J. Ulrich

109

Nuthatches (Family Sittidae) live among tree trunks and larger branches. These small birds have short tails, long wings and long, slightly upturned bills. Nuthatches glean the bark for insects, spiders and larvae and also eat the nuts and seeds of conifers. An enlarged hind toe enables them to hunt head-down and find insects overlooked by other birds. Nuthatches are monogamous, defend territories year-round and lay five to nine eggs in cavity nests. Suet and sunflower seeds easily attract them to bird feeders.

Red-breasted Nuthatch *Sitta canadensis*

Field marks: 4½"; small size; black crown; black eyeline; white eyebrow; **rufous underparts**.
Status: fairly common resident throughout the region and in RMNP.

These birds inhabit open stands of lodgepole and Douglas fir at higher elevations. Red-breasted nuthatches excavate nesting cavities in conifers or conifer snags and smear the entrance holes with pitch. The birds fly directly into the hole without perching or pausing at the entrance.

White-breasted Nuthatch *Sitta carolinensis*

Field marks: 6"; black crown; **white face and underparts**; blue-gray back.
Status: fairly common resident in deciduous habitats throughout the region and in RMNP.

The largest of the nuthatches, the white-breasted occupies a wide variety of habitats. These birds rub insects around the entrance holes to their nests. Once identified, its loud "yank-yank" call is easy to recognize.

Pygmy Nuthatch *Sitta pygmaea*

Field marks: 4½"; brownish head; **black eyeline**; bluish-gray back.
Status: local resident in drier habitats of the southern half of the region; common in RMNP.

The smallest of the nuthatches, the pygmy searches the clusters of pine needles at the ends of the branches for insects and pine seeds. The quiet habits and soft twittering voice of this friendly bird make it an inconspicuous resident of yellow pine habitats. Because of its small size, it can nest in cavities too small for other species to use.

Creepers (Family Certhiidae) are small birds that probe the bark of trees for small insects and insect larvae with their long slender decurved bills. Like woodpeckers, they brace themselves with their tails when feeding.

Brown Creeper *Certhia americana*

Field marks: 5"; small size; brownish above, streaked with white; white below; **fine, decurved bill**; sharp claws; **long pointed tail**.
Status: fairly common resident of forested areas of the region and in RMNP.

Brown creepers inhabit coniferous forests where they feed mostly on bark insects which they find by spiralling up a tree trunk, dropping to the base of the next one and beginning the spiral ascent again. They wedge their nests under a loose slab of bark.

Red-breasted Nuthatch
T. J. Ulrich

White-breasted Nuthatch
T. J. Ulrich

Pygmy Nuthatch   T. J. Ulrich

Brown Creeper   E. T. Jones

Wrens (Family Troglodytidae) are small, brown, active birds with slender bills that feed almost exclusively on insects. Recognize these birds easily by their habit of cocking their tail over their back and their loud, pleasing songs. Wrens build their nests in cavities, in crevices or in reeds. They prefer to remain hidden in thickets but become very bold when intruders venture too close to their nests.

Rock Wren *Salpinctes obsoletus*

Field marks: 5"; long, thin bill; gray brown above; **long tail with buff tips**.

Status: common summer residents throughout the drier rocky areas of the region and RMNP.

Although common, rock wrens are relatively difficult to find. They inhabit rocky washes where they probe cracks and crevices for insects and spiders. They tuck their nests, built of fine plant materials and lined with fur or feathers, into rock crevices where they are hidden and protected. They often place small pebbles at the entrance to the crevice. Intruders into the territories face persistent scolding.

House Wren *Troglodytes aedon*

Field marks: 5"; gray-brown above; pale brown below; slender bill; **barred tail**; *Voice*-a rapidly rising and falling bubbly trill.

Status: common summer residents throughout the region and in RMNP

House wrens, the most common of the wrens, are cavity nesters with a reputation for nesting in strange places: an old tin can, a cow skull, a pump spigot, the pocket of a discarded coat or a mail box. Common wherever there are sufficient thickets—in open stands of trees, near forest edges, in old orchards and near old trees and rundown buildings—wrens aggressively compete for nesting cavities. They may puncture the eggs of other birds in the process of evicting them. The males attract the females by singing and by filling as many as twelve nesting cavities with sticks. Once the female decides on a mate, she throws the sticks out of the cavity of her choice and does things her own way. Very vocal, house wrens sing their beautiful songs any and all times of day.

Marsh Wren *Cistothorus palustris*

Field marks: 5"; brown plumage; **solid rufous crown; white eyebrow**; long de-curved bill; white-streaked back.

Status: common summer residents in suitable habitat throughout the region and in RMNP.

As their name implies, marsh wrens are conspicuous residents of cattail and bulrush marshes and wet roadside ditches. After building numerous (up to 35 in some cases) domed nests to attract a female, the males perch high on a rush or cattail and launch their sputtery calls and trills. Once won over, the female moves into one of the nests, leaving the rest vacant. Although most marsh wrens move to Mexico and the southern border states for the winter, some do remain in the region year-round.

Rock Wren   T. J. Ulrich

House Wren   J. L. Wassink

Marsh Wren   J. L. Wassink

Dippers (Family Cinclidae) orient their lives almost completely around the water. Extremely soft, thick plumage and an exceptionally large preen gland allow them to treat cold temperatures and icy water with impunity. A moveable flap that covers the nostrils, a nictitating membrane over the eyes and strong feet and legs to grasp the rocky bottom enable the dipper to forage underwater for aquatic insects and insect larvae. (They also use their wings to help hold them on the bottom, which has led some writers to report that these birds "fly" underwater.)

American Dipper   *Cinclus mexicanus*

> **Field marks:** 8"; small, **plump; slate gray**; short stubby tail; **bobs up and down.**
>
> **Status:** common resident along the rushing, tumbling, icy cold mountain streams of the region and in RMNP.

Even on extremely cold winter days, these birds wade in shallow riffles, disappearing under the ice in search of aquatic insects and tiny fish. When flying to foraging areas either upstream or downstream, the dipper flies over the water, seldom taking shortcuts over land. The female constructs the bulky ball of a nest out of moss with a side entrance and always locates it near the water—on a rock wall, under a bridge or even behind a waterfall. Frequently, the nest lies where a constant spray from the water keeps the moss damp and alive, forming a living, growing nest. The dipper's melodious song is pleasant, when it can be heard over the roar of the water.

Kinglets (Family Muscicapidae, Subfamily Sylviinae) are tiny active insect eaters. Flighty birds, they forage near the ground but nest in the tree-tops of conifers, often Douglas firs. The deep semi-pensile nest is tucked in the fork of a horizontal branch and well hidden in the needles. Kinglets lay eight or nine eggs—a large clutch for such small birds.

Ruby-crowned Kinglet   *Regulus calendula*

> **Field marks:** 4¼"; small size; olive-green above; small thin bill; **broken white eye-ring**; two white wing bars; male-red crown patch (visible only when excited).
>
> **Status:** fairly common summer resident in suitable habitat throughout the region and in RMNP.

One of the smallest of the songbirds, the ruby-crowned kinglet inhabits coniferous forests where it flits and hops among the twigs and leaves in pursuit of insects. Its song, "liberty, liberty, liberty," is very loud for such a small singer and is audible at great distances. The male reveals his red crown patch only when he is excited. The only other North American kinglet, the golden-crowned kinglet, has an orange crown edged with black and frequents primarily spruce-fir forests at higher elevations in the central Rockies.

American Dipper   T. J. Ulrich

American Dipper   T. J. Ulrich

Ruby-crowned Kinglet   E. T. Jones

115

Thrushes (Family Muscicapidae, Subfamily Turdinae) are small- to medium-sized songbirds that live on a mixed diet of insects, invertebrates and plant materials. Nests are cup-shaped structures built in the crotch of a tree or in a cavity. Singing ability is highly variable—while some can barely twitter, others are marvelous songsters.

Western Bluebird   *Sialia mexicana*

Field marks: 6"; *male*-deep blue back, throat and wings; **rusty breast; chestnut patch on upper back**; hunched appearance; *female*-grayish; rust tint to breast; bluish wings and tail.

Status: fairly common to unusual summer resident throughout the region and in RMNP.

The main concern for the future of these inhabitants of open timber lands is the loss of nesting cavities through logging, replacement of wooden fenceposts by metal fenceposts and competition with starlings, wrens, tree swallows and sparrows. Concerned birders can counteract this problem by providing birdhouses. Like the other bluebirds, western bluebirds feed mainly on insects that they hawk from the air or pick from the ground.

Mountain Bluebird   *Sialia currucoides*

Field marks: 6½"; *male*-**sky blue plumage**; *female*-duller gray with blue tinge on wings.

Status: common summer resident throughout the region and in RMNP.

Mountain bluebirds arrive in the area early, often when there is still snow on the ground. They select an open territory near a dead snag or suitable nesting cavity in sagebrush-grassland or mountain meadow habitats. As with the western bluebird, the availability of nesting cavities limits its distribution. In areas with suitable open spaces, putting up nest boxes can increase populations dramatically. Mountain bluebirds snap up insects, their main food, from the ground or out of the air. Bluebirds often hover when pursuing insects. In fall and winter, berries add to the diet. After the raising the young, often two broods, the family groups join large flocks before heading south.

Townsend's Solitaire   *Myadestes townsendi*

Field marks: 9"; slim build; **white eye-ring**; gray plumage; **pale salmon wing patches**; long white tail; quiet, shy behavior.

Status: fairly common summer resident throughout the region and in RMNP.

Look for Townsend's solitaire perched on the outermost or topmost branches of a small tree along the edge of a small clearing in the high coniferous forests—often an open pine and fir or juniper forest. From these perches, they hawk insects like the flycatchers or utter their single pipping note. They build their nests on or near the ground—in a sheltered hollow, under an overhang in a cut bank or sheltered by a log or stone. The eggs are white and heavily blotched. Townsend's solitaires sing their beautiful song, consisting of a long series of rapidly warbled loud clear notes, from the tops of tall trees or while in flight.

Male and female Western Bluebirds   J. L. Wassink

Mountain Bluebird   J. L. Wassink

Townsend's Solitaire   J. L. Wassink

Swainson's Thrush   *Catharus ustulatus*

Field marks: 7"; olive brown back; **buffy face and eye ring**; white below; spotted buff breast.

Status: common throughout the region and in RMNP.

These inhabitants of large stands of mixed conifers and deciduous brush and trees carry on their activities quietly and are often overlooked. Swainson's thrushes sing their ascending flute-like song at dawn and again at dusk. The rest of the day, they feed on the ground, searching through the forest litter for worms, grubs and invertebrates. They also feed on berries when available. They build their nests in the crotch of a tree. After raising the brood, they ready themselves for the long migration to South America.

Hermit Thrush   *Catharus guttatus*

Field marks: 7"; olive brown back; buffy face and eye ring; white below; spotted buff breast; **reddish-brown tail**.

Status: fairly common summer resident throughout the region.

The hermit thrush prefers the heavy foliage, deep shadows and damp areas of the region—willow thickets, river woods and forest undergrowth of mixed conifers and aspen. Some characterize its serene flute-like song as the most beautiful sound in nature. Although the hermit thrush goes south like the rest of the thrushes, it stops in the southern tier of states from Florida to southern California, making it the only thrush that normally winters in the United States.

American Robin   *Turdus migratorius*

Field marks: 10"; plump profile; black head; yellow bill; dark gray-brown back; **dark red-orange breast**.

Status: abundant resident throughout the region and in RMNP.

Robins frequent virtually all habitats in the region except marshes.Very adaptable birds, they become tame in the lawns and gardens of cities but remain extremely shy in the wilderness and remote alpine regions. Robins feed on worms, insects and fruit (cherries, apples, mountain ash and cotoneaster). They build their sturdy grass-lined nest in the crotch of a tree and lay up to six turquoise blue eggs. The young grow quickly. By the time they leave the nest, they closely resemble the adults, except for their densely spotted breasts. Immediately after the first brood leaves the nest, the adults build another nest and raise a second brood.

Swainson's Thrush   J. L. Wassink

American Robin   J. L. Wassink

Hermit Thrush   E. T. Jones

119

Mockingbirds (Family Mimidae) are superb songsters and are highly territorial. They inhabit open brushy country and often sing from a conspicuous perch. Their neutral colors—grays, slaty or plain brown—provide camouflage while they build their basin-shaped nests and incubate three to six blue, green or grayish eggs. The family names "Mimidae" and "Mockingbirds" comes from the amazing ability these birds have to mimic the songs of other birds.

Gray Catbird   *Dumetella crolinensis*

> **Field marks:** 9"; plain slaty gray; **black cap; rusty undertail coverts**; sings notes of song only once.
> **Status:** fairly common throughout the region and in RMNP

Quiet and unobtrusive, gray catbirds are seldom seen by anyone not looking for them. Even then, only their soft "mew" call betrays their presence in thick brushy streamside areas. They utter this call, which gives them their name, when they are disturbed. Catbirds have a varied repertoire of songs that they sing any time of day and even at night. Insects make up roughly half of their diet but they also eat fruit and berries. They fashion their rough nests low in a tangle of vines, a dense hedge or in a mass of garden shrubs. The usual clutch consists of four greenish-blue eggs.

Sage Thrasher   *Oreoscoptes montanus*

> **Field marks:** 9"; short straight bill; gray-brown above; **heavily streaked breast**; white-tipped tail.
> **Status:** local summer resident in sagebrush habitats throughout the region and in RMNP.

Listen for the sage thrasher's loud, long, beautiful song in the dry sagebrush deserts of the region in early summer. The source of the song can often be spotted perched on a tall sage or flying in large circles over the sage flats. Sage thrashers hunt on the ground like robins and consume large numbers of grasshoppers.

Brown Thrasher   *Toxostoma rufum*

> **Field marks:** 11"; large size; yellow eyes; brown-rufous above; **buff-white streaked breast**; long tail; repeats notes of song twice.
> **Status:** rare west of the divide and in RMNP; more common east of the divide.

Like the other thrashers, the brown thrasher is a rather shy bird that frequents dense cover. You may often hear this skilled singer but seldom see it. When feeding, it digs with its bill through the forest litter and sometimes even into the ground in search of insects. It also eats berries, fruits, nuts and corn.

Gray Catbird   J. L. Wassink

Sage Thrasher   J. L. Wassink

Brown Thrasher   T. J. Ulrich

Wagtails (Family Motacillidae) are a predominantly Old World family of small, slender birds with long tails, long legs, long toes and elongated claws. Their plumage is inconspicuous but the birds' elaborate in-flight courtship displays make them highly visible.

Water Pipit   *Anthus spinoletta*

Field marks: 6½"; **slender profile**; slender bill; brown back; white, lightly streaked underparts; white outer tail feathers; long hind claw; **wags tail as it walks**.

Status: summer resident in the region and in RMNP.

The alpine tundra is the summer home of these birds. There, the male sings his courtship song high in the air and then floats back to the ground on fluttering wings. The female builds the nest on the ground, usually in the shelter of overhanging vegetation or nestled beside a rock. When fall comes to the high country, water pipits move to the lowlands to winter on bare fields, mud flats and beaches. Water pipits feed by walking about plucking insects and seeds from the ground and vegetation. The call is a two-syllabled "pipit."

Larks (Family Alaudidae) inhabit the short-grass prairies and other areas with short sparse grasses. They walk when on the ground, feed on insects or seeds, and build their cup-shaped nests under a tuft of grass. Of particular note is the lark's flight songs, which they utter from as high as 800 feet above the ground.

Horned Lark   *Eremophila alpestris*

Field marks: 8"; brown above; white below; **black crown, facial stripe and breast band**; slender bill; horns not always visible

Status: an abundant resident in the short grass/sagebrush/alpine tundra areas throughout the region and in RMNP

The horned lark nests in wide expanses of open country—short sparse grasslands and alpine tundra—where it digs or finds a slight hollow to contain two to five finely speckled off-white eggs. While courting, the male sometimes sings its weak song from a perch on the ground but also sings while circling high above the ground, sometimes as high as 800 feet. The horned lark walks instead of hopping like many birds and seldom perches in trees or shrubs. When feeding, it walks or runs over the ground in search of weed seeds, waste grain and insects.

Water Pipit   E. T. Jones

Horned Lark   W. Shattil & R. Rozinski

123

Waxwings (Family Bombycillidae) are gregarious birds that live in flocks for most of the year. They perch, feed and fly in squadrons. Waxwings have prominent crests, soft silky plumage in drab colors and were named waxwings because of the waxy tips on the wing coverts. They have adapted short stout bills for eating fruit and their sturdy legs and feet allow them to stretch in all directions without falling to reach the fruit. Monogamous, they court by passing berries or other objects back and forth. Their weak songs have no known function in courtship. Waxwings perch their well-built nests out on a high branch and lay three to five bluish-gray eggs. They nest later than most birds and feed their young berries and fruit. Occasionally, in late winter, they eat fermented fruit and exhibit signs of intoxication.

Bohemian Waxwing   *Bombycilla garrulus*

Field marks: 8"; pale gray plumage; black mask; **crest; red waxy tips on wing coverts**; yellow and **white spots in wings**; chestnut undertail coverts.

Status: irregular winter visitor in northern part of the region; even less frequent in the southern part of the region and in RMNP.

Larger, grayer, and with a more northern distribution than cedar waxwings, Bohemian waxwings inhabit open conifer and mixed woodlands where they build their nests in conifers. These birds often pass inedible objects, such as sticks or pebbles, back and forth in courtship displays. In summer, they sometimes hawk insects out of the air like flycatchers. Nomadic in winter, they travel erratically in search of plentiful supplies of berries, sometimes wandering far south of their normal range.

Cedar Waxwing   *Bombycilla cedrorum*

Field marks: 7"; pale brown plumage; black mask; **crest; red waxy tips on wing coverts; yellow tipped tail**.

Status: fairly common summer resident in northern Wyoming and Idaho, less common in Colorado and Utah; rare summer visitor in RMNP; irregular winter visitor throughout the region.

An inhabitant of brushlands mixed with second growth timber, cedar waxwings often hawk insects from a conspicuous perch like flycatchers. The call is a high pitched "zee." The courtship display usually involves exchanging an edible object, such as a berry or petal, and ends when one of the birds eats the object. The female builds the nest in a conifer or deciduous bush. Depending on where they locate an abundant supply of berries or fruit, cedar waxwings may winter anywhere from southern Canada to Panama. Squadrons of these birds often descend on cities and feed on the berries of ornamental trees.

Bohemian Waxwing   J. L. Wassink

Cedar Waxwing   J. L. Wassink

Cedar Waxwing   J. L. Wassink

125

Shrikes (Family Lannidae) are songbirds that act like birds of prey. They feed on large insects, small lizards, mice and small birds, which they kill with their powerful hook-tipped bill. Like the birds of prey, shrikes have powerful feet to help them tear their meal into bite-sized pieces. If prey is not consumed immediately, they impale it on a thorn or barbed wire for later.

Loggerhead Shrike   *Lanius ludovicianus*

Field marks: 9"; gray, white and black plumage; **heavy, hooked bill**; big head; broad black mask that meets over bill; rapid wingbeats; long thin tail.

Status: fairly common summer residents throughout CR; rare in RMNP.

Loggerhead shrikes most often dwell in open country where you can see them sitting quietly on telephone wires beside the road or perching on the highest twig of a tree or bush. From these perches they search the ground for any movement that might betray the presence of a mouse, small bird or large insect. Once a shrike captures its prey, the bird either immediately eats it, feeds it to the nestlings, or stores it for later use by impaling it on a nearby thorn bush or barbed wire fence. Both sexes assist in building the bulky nest, which they usually locate deep in a low bush, to provide a home for four to seven youngsters.

Starlings (Family Sturnidae) were brought to New York from Europe by a man who wanted to introduce to North America all the birds mentioned by Shakespeare. Starlings have displaced other birds such as bluebirds and swallows from nesting cavities and have proliferated. This ability to displace other, more colorful and tamer birds has not endeared the starling to modern birders. Starlings have stout straight bills and large strong feet and legs—equipment ideally suited to a bird who feeds on virtually anything it can locate while walking on the ground.

European Starling   *Sturnus vulgaris*

Field marks: 8"; plump; glossy black iridescent plumage; **long yellow bill**; **short tail**; walks with a waddle; *winter*-spotted with dark bill.

Status: abundant resident or summer resident throughout the region and in RMNP.

These adaptable European immigrants inhabit cities or short grass farmlands with nearby cavities for nest sites. They lay four to six blue or bluish-white eggs. These much despised birds very aggressively compete for nesting cavities, displacing native species of bluebirds and swallows—birds that many people prefer to starlings. Far from musical, their seemingly ceaseless calling and squabbling consists of various squeaks, chirps and whistles. Starlings usually gather their highly variable diet of insects, cherries, and seeds from the ground. In fall and winter, they join in huge flocks to feed and roost. The huge communal roosts are usually considered a nuisance wherever they are located.

Loggerhead Shrike   J. L. Wassink

Loggerhead Shrike   T. J. Ulrich

European Starling   J. L. Wassink

127

Vireos (Family Vireonidae) are small plain birds that are difficult to observe but easy to hear. "Vireo" literally means "I am green," which suits this family well. They sport a stout bill with a slight hook on the upper mandible. Deliberate birds, vireos feed on insects that they pluck off the foliage of the understory. The nest, a neat basket decorated with bits of lichen, sits in the fork of a sapling and holds two to five white eggs. Both sexes help incubate the eggs and feed the young. Persistent songsters, the males of some of the species may even sing from the nest while taking their turn incubating the eggs.

Warbling Vireo   *Vireo gilvus*

Field marks: 5½"; light gray above; whitish eyebrow; whitish below; **no wing bars**.

Status: fairly common summer resident throughout the region and in RMNP.

Alder thickets and open deciduous woodlands are where you will find this inconspicuous bird. The warbling vireo moves deliberately through the undergrowth as it gleans insects from the foliage. The male accompanies the female as she builds nest, singing along the way, but he does not help her with the construction. The female lines the well-made nest with fine grasses and then suspends it from a fork in a small tree. The distinctive, husky, warbling song of this vireo often ends on a rising note.

Red-eyed Vireo   *Vireo olivaceus*

Field marks: 6"; olive-green above; gray crown; **white eyebrow with black borders**; dark eyeline; red eyes; whitish below.

Status: local summer resident and migrant throughout the region; rare in RMNP.

Although this bird is the most common bird of the eastern deciduous forests, it is not nearly as abundant here in the central Rockies. The red-eyed vireo frequents streamside deciduous trees and aspen-poplar groves. Its almost continuous singing has lead to the nickname "preacher-bird." Both sexes build the nest but the female incubates the eggs alone. Like the other vireos, the red-eyed feeds by gleaning insects as it works its way through the undergrowth. This vireo migrates as far as 3,000 miles to winter in the Amazon basin of South America. There it forms small flocks that move from one fruiting tree to another.

Warbling Vireo   J. L. Wassink

Red-eyed Vireo   J. L. Wassink

Warblers (Family Emberizidae, Subfamily Parulinae) are small often brightly colored birds that pick insects from leaves and twigs of trees and shrubs with their slender, pointed bills. Some frequent the forest floor, others reeds, still others brushy stream sides and others the tree tops. Intensely territorial, they defend their turf with their thin wiry songs. They build their cup-shaped nests in the fork of a branch and lay from three to six eggs. The males are often brightly colored, the females duller. Warblers migrate to Mexico and South America in winter. The ongoing destruction of their wintering grounds poses an extremely serious threat to the population stability of these birds.

Yellow Warbler *Dendroica petechia*

Field marks: 5"; *male*-orange-yellow plumage; rusty streaks on breast; *female*-yellow-green plumage.

Status: common summer resident throughout the region and in RMNP.

Yellow warblers are the best known and most widely distributed of the warblers. They inhabit streamside thickets of willow, alder and cottonwood. Within those thickets, they seek out caterpillars, cankerworms, "measuring worms," moth larvae, bark beetles, weevils and similar creatures. Brown-headed cowbirds often parasitize yellow warblers by laying their eggs in the warbler's nest. If the warbler discovers the addition, it may construct a new floor over the cowbird egg and begin a new clutch of its own.

Yellow-rumped Warbler *Dendroica coronata*

Field marks: 5"; *male*-dark gray plumage; **yellow patches on crown, throat,** sides and rump; white wing patches; *female*-grayish-brown plumage.

Status: common summer breeder throughout the region and in RMNP.

The yellow-rumped warbler dwells in the twigs and branches of medium-sized trees where it is usually in perpetual motion—darting, flitting, hanging upside down and hawking insects out of the air. It inhabits mixed woods and usually nests in the top of a conifer. This species consists of two varieties that interbreed where their breeding ranges meet. The bird found in this area is called "Audubon's Warbler" and can be distinquished by its yellow throat. It breeds in the central Rockies as well as north and west throughout the western mountains. It winters in the lowlands along the Pacific coast and the gulf of Mexico. The other variety, the "Myrtle Warbler," whose range is largely in the eastern United States, has a white throat and white spots on its crown and sides.

Male Yellow Warbler   J. L. Wassink

Female Yellow Warbler   J. L. Wassink

Yellow-rumped Warbler (Audubon's Warbler)   J. L. Wassink

American Redstart
Setophaga ruticilla

Field marks: 5"; *male*-**black plumage**; orange marks on tail, wings and breast; *female*-olive and yellow with salmon marks on wing.
Status: fairly common summer resident throughout the region and in RMNP.

Trees, abundant brush and water are the common components of the American redstart's habitat. This bird often seeks out second growth woodlands and streamside alder and willow thickets. Highly insectivorous, the American redstart hunts below the forest canopy, often hawking insects out of the air like a flycatcher. The young male gets the black and orange color pattern of the adult male in their second year. The nest usually sits close to the ground in the crotch of a tree. Brown-headed cowbirds often parasitize American redstart nests.

Common Yellowthroat
Geothlypis trichas

Field marks: 5"; small size; olive-brown above; **black mask; yellow throat**; *female*-olive-brown above; yellow throat.
Status: common summer resident throughout the region and in RMNP.

Yellowthroats are common inhabitants of heavy, damp shrubbery and brushy undergrowth, usually near open water. Highly territorial like wrens, they scold trespassers on the territory loudly. Because of their dense habitat and shy nature, the yellowthroats' call—"witchety, witchety, witchety"—is often the only way to detect them. The birds build their extremely well-hidden nests near or on the ground. They feed by gleaning insects from the leaves of shrubs, grasses and weeds. Like many of the other wood warblers, yellowthroats are often victims of a cowbird's egg deposit.

Yellow-breasted Chat
Icteria virens

Field marks: 7½"; large size; olive-green above; **heavy black bill**; white eye-ring; yellow throat and breast; **long tail**.
Status: fairly common throughout the lower elevations of the region; vagrant only in RMNP.

Similar at first glance to the common yellowthroat except for its size, the yellow-breasted chat prefers dense deciduous streamsides and the margins of moist meadows. This noisy bird is the largest wood warbler and one of the most secretive. Often, the only clues to its presence are the repeated alternating sequence of clear whistles and harsh notes. Like most of the wood warblers, yellow-breasted chats winter in Mexico and Central America.

Male American Redstart
J. L. Wassink

Male Common Yellow Throat
J. L. Wassink

Yellow-breasted Chat   T. J. Ulrich

133

Tanagers (Family Emberizidae, Subfamily Thraupidae) are predominantly tropical birds—of 242 species, only a couple wander into the temperate habitats of the world. The males have brilliantly colored plumage and both sexes sport stout bills. They are monogamous and most sing either weak songs or no songs at all. Tanagers eat insects, fruit and nectar.

Western Tanager   *Piranga ludoviciana*

Field marks: 7"; *male*-**black and yellow plumage**; stout bill; **orange-red head**; black wings and tail; one yellow and one white wing bar; *female*-yellow-gray plumage; stout bill; gray back; two thin wing bars.
Status: fairly common summer resident in coniferous habitats throughout the region and in RMNP.

These brightly colored summer visitors inhabit open conifers, mixed spruce and fir forests, lodgepole pine forests, and Douglas fir-aspen habitats up to 10,000 feet throughout the region. They search the treetops for caterpillars and insects. Quiet feeders, they do some flycatching from high limbs but usually simply glean insects they chance upon while moving quietly through the upper branches. Tanagers often place their shallow saucerlike nest in a fork near the end of a branch midway up an evergreen tree. The male does not incubate but does help feed the young. Its casual song, drifting down from the treetops, is a common sound in the central Rockies and often the most easily detected sign of the tanager's presence. With the approach of winter and the subsequent decline in insect populations, they migrate to Mexico and Costa Rica. Attract tanagers to feeders with supplies of dried fruit, oranges and cake.

Buntings and Finches (Family Emberizidae, Subfamily Coerebinae) are small, seed-eating birds. Their conical bills are pointed at the tip for picking up seeds and heavy at the base for cracking them. Buntings and finches live in all habitats in the region and vary from dull to brilliantly colored. Their songs are generally beautiful.

Lazuli Bunting   *Passerina amoena*

Field marks: 6"; *male*-blue head; **stubby bill**; blue back and wings; orange-brown breast and flanks; **white wing bars**; white belly; *female*-grayish-brown above; buff below; pale wing bars.
Status: fairly common to common summer resident throughout the region and in RMNP.

Lazuli buntings are birds of shrubbery, thickets and tangled second growth timber, often near streamsides. There, they sing from exposed perches while nervously flicking their tails. In addition to seeds, they sometimes eat insects that they hunt on the ground. They place the nest, woven of coarse grasses and lined with finer materials and hair, low in the shrubbery. The female incubates the four eggs alone, but is assisted by the male while feeding the young.

Male Western Tanager

Female Western Tanager

Lazuli Bunting

135

Towhees and Sparrows (Family Emberizidae, Subfamily
Emberizinae) are small (four to seven inches) birds with predominantly dull
gray or brown plumage. Differentiate these birds primarily on the basis of
subtle but distinctive plumage such as face, crown or breast pattern. One or
more sparrows occupy all habitats in the region.

Green-tailed Towhee   *Pipilo chlorurus*

Field marks: 7"; slender; gray-green above; **rufous cap**; white throat.
Status: fairly common summer resident in the brushy transitional habitats
of the region and in RMNP.

Detect these secretive birds as they sing from an exposed perch. Their
song consists of a peculiar cat-like mew note or a series of clear notes
followed by a coarse trill. Green-tailed towhees feed on the ground beneath
the low bushes of open mountainsides or high sagebrush plains. They
scratch for insects and seeds by simultaneously kicking back with both feet.
When disturbed, they fly low to the ground while pumping their tails.
Attract them to feeders with bread, birdseed or grain.

Rufous-sided Towhee   *Pipilo erythrophthalmus*

Field marks: 8"; black hood and back; white spots on wings; **rufous sides
and flanks**; flashing white tail patches.
Status: fairly common summer resident in all but the drier areas of the
region; migrant in RMNP.

Open woods and undergrowth provide cover for the rufous-sided towhee
as it feeds among the dead leaves, kicking with both feet at once. Its rather
unmusical song says its name—"tow-eee." This towhee locates its nest
either on the ground or low in a dense bush. The western variant of this
widely distributed species has numerous white spots on its back.

Brown Towhee   *Pipilo fuscus*

Field marks: 9"; dull, plain gray-brown plumage; buffy striped throat;
long tail; **cinnamon or rust undertail coverts**.
Status: Fairly common resident in the extreme southern part of the
region; vagrant only farther north; rare resident in RMNP.

Inhabitants of the cholla cactus and pinyon-juniper country and other
shrublands of southern Colorado, brown towhees also occasionally show up
in suburban gardens. Not as vigorous or visible in their foraging as the
rufous-sided towhee, these birds emerge only rarely from dense shady cover
where they quietly search for tasty tidbits. Strongly territorial, brown
towhees are believed to mate for life. The bulky nest of twigs and grasses
lined with strips of bark, leaves and hair usually sits in a tree or shrub from
two to ten, but sometimes up to 35, feet above the ground.

Green-tailed Towhee J. L. Wassink

Rufous-sided Towhee W. Shattil & R. Rozinski

Brown Towhee J. L. Wassink

American Tree Sparrow   *Spizella arborea*

Field marks: 6"; **chestnut crown**; dark upper mandible; yellow lower mandible; white wing bars; **grayish breast with central dark spot.**

Status: fairly common migrant and abundant winter resident throughout the region; less abundant in RMNP.

After spending the summer breeding in the arctic scrub of northern Canada and Alaska where they establish large territories of up to two and a half acres, American tree sparrows move south to the central Rockies to pass the winter. Watch for these birds in open country perching on shrubs or small trees or foraging in small bands along brushy roadsides, weedy edges and marshes.

Chipping Sparrow   *Spizella passerina*

Field marks: 5½"; **solid rufous crown; white eyebrow**; black eyeline; unstreaked gray below.

Status: common summer resident throughout the region and in RMNP.

Chipping sparrows are small, tame birds that occupy open areas in dry environments with thinly scattered trees. Their name comes from their song: a series of rapid chips that they usually deliver from the outermost branches of a tree. The nest is a hairlined cup on a conifer branch. Chipping sparrows feed on seeds and insects that they search for either on or close to the ground.

Lark Sparrow   *Chondestes grammacus*

Field marks: 6"; streaked brown above; **bold rufous, white and black head pattern**; black central tail feathers; white corners and outer tail feathers.

Status: fairly common to abundant throughout the grassland habitats of the region; common in RMNP.

You will find these boldly colored sparrows in dry open meadows. During migration, they gather in large flocks in weedy fields and along roadsides where they search for insects and seeds. One of our finest singers, its song is a series of long liquid trills and phrases. The lark sparrow conceals its nest in dense vegetation on the ground.

American Tree Sparrow

Chipping Sparrow

Lark Sparrow

139

Black-throated Sparrow   *Amphispiza bilineata*

Field marks: 5"; black and gray plumage; dark gray crown; white eyebrow; **black throat** with white borders; white below.

Status: rare local summer resident in dry upland habitats throughout the region; not found in RMNP.

Look for black-throated sparrows in scattered cactus, yucca or mesquite habitats interspersed with sparse grasses. In these areas, they seek out dense thickets of low bushes and shrubs for protection and for concealing their nests. Adapted to desert conditions, black-throated sparrows get their moisture from the seeds and insects they consume.

Lark Bunting   *Calamospiza melanocorys*

Field marks: 7"; *male*-**black body; white wing patches;** *female*-streaked brown plumage; brown cheek patch; **pale wing patches**.

Status: an abundant summer resident in the eastern part of the region; local in western part; migrant in RMNP.

Lark buntings inhabit the tall grass prairies and plains. Year after year, the males return to the same territories and try to attract one or more females by flying up in the air a few yards and then uttering their songs while slowly circling back to the ground on uptilted wings. The arriving females soon settle into the territories of their choice and construct well-hidden nests, lined with hair, moss, wool or feathers, on the ground . Since the polygamous male may have several females in his territory, the female is left to incubate alone. However, once the young have hatched, the male may assist with the feeding.

Savannah Sparrow   *Passerculus sandwichensis*

Field marks: 6"; brown streaked plumage; **narrow, yellow eyebrow; notched tail**.

Status: fairly common summer resident throughout the region and in RMNP.

Throughout the spring, the savannah sparrow sings its weak, lispy song near moist grassy sites all the way up to timberline. In spite of inhabiting open country, these small, nondescript birds are secretive and hard to see and identify. When disturbed, they take to the air in a short erratic flight but soon drop back to the ground and vanish by running through the grass. Savannah sparrows build their nests in grass-lined hollows in short-grass or sparse vegetation such as the grassy fringe of a marsh. Depending on the season, they eat insects or seeds. In winter, they move south far enough to avoid the snow.

Black-throated Sparrow   J. L. Wassink

Lark Bunting   J. L. Wassink

Savannah Sparrow   J. L. Wassink

141

Fox Sparrow   *Passerella iliaca*

Field marks: 7"; **large size**; grayish-brown plumage: **heavily blotched breast**; large dark spot in middle of breast; **rufous tinge in tail**.
Status: unusual summer resident throughout the region and in RMNP.

The largest sparrow, the fox sparrow forages among the dead leaves of underbrush by kicking back with both feet at once. Stunted conifers at timberline, shrubby avalanche slopes and dense thickets in the subalpine regions provide the heavy cover this bird loves. In winter, the fox sparrow frequents the brushy undergrowths in the valleys.

Song Sparrow   *Melospiza melodia*

Field marks: 6½"; heavily streaked brown plumage; **large central breast spot**.
Status: fairly common resident throughout the region and in RMNP.

One of the first birds of spring, song sparrows arrive before the snow melts. Tolerant of human activities, these birds prefer the cover of shrubbery, hedgerows, brushlands and forest edges where they feed on the ground, scratching with both feet at once. When flitting from one bush to another, they often dip their tails. Their cheerful and persistent singing and their rich and varied repertoire of songs puts song sparrows in the running for the top singer of the bird world. Almost fifty years ago, song sparrows were the subject of a behavioral study by Margaret Nice. She traced their life history from territory establishment and defense by the male to pair bonding, courtship, breeding behavior, nesting and feeding behavior.

White-throated Sparrow   *Zonotrichia albicollis*

Field marks: 7"; brown plumage streaked with black; black and white striped head; **yellow lores**; **white throat**; gray breast.
Status: rare migrant throughout the region and in RMNP.

Because they nest in Canada, as far north as the treeline, white-throated sparrows pass through here only during the spring and fall migrations. Look for these ground feeders along the margins of deciduous and mixed forests as they scratch noisily beneath the brush for insects, weed seeds and wild fruits. Their beautiful song has been "translated" as "Old Sam Peabody, Peabody, Peabody."

Fox Sparrow   J. L. Wassink

Song Sparrow   J. L. Wassink

White-throated Sparrow   T. J. Ulrich

143

White-crowned Sparrow — *Zonotrichia leucophrys*

Field marks: 6½"; grayish back streaked with black and brown; **black and white striped crown**; gray face, neck and breast; pink bill; long tail.
Status: fairly common to common resident throughout the region and in RMNP.

White-crowned sparrows inhabit dense thickets of shrubs interspersed with open feeding areas, such as the willow thickets of mountain meadows and along the margins of lakes. The nest is a grass-lined cup on the ground or in the fork of a low willow or conifer. When disturbed, these sparrows utter a metallic "pink." Attract them to bird feeders with mixed seeds.

Chestnut-collared Longspur — *Calcarius ornatus*

Field marks: 6½"; black breast and underparts; chestnut nape patch; mostly white tail with black terminal triangle; long hind toenail.
Status: summer resident on plains; local migrant throughout the region; rare migrant in RMNP.

Inhabitants of short-grass habitats, chestnut-collared longspurs frequent grazed or mown grasslands and pastures where they feed on weed seeds. Their conspicuous flight song resembles the song of the meadowlark. Chestnut-collared longspurs nest on the ground, concealed in a clump of grasses.

Snow Bunting — *Plectrophenax nivalis*

Field marks: 7"; *summer*-white head and belly; black back; *winter*-mottled buff, white and black plumage; white belly; *in flight*-**large white wing patches**.
Status: rare winter migrant in the southern part of the region and in RMNP; more common in the north.

One of the most northern nesters, snow buntings spend their summers in northern Canada. After raising their young, they remain in the north until forced to move south when snow covers the weed seeds they survive on. Among the most cold tolerant of the small birds, snow buntings gather in large flocks and move only far enough south to find snow-free prairies and fields suitable for feeding. Look for them along windswept roadsides in open country.

White-crowned Sparrow   J. L. Wassink

Chestnut-collared Longspur   T. J. Ulrich

Snow Bunting   A. G. Nelson

145

Dark-eyed Junco   *Junco hyemalis*

Field marks: 6"; sparrow-sized; light pink bill; dark eyes; gray or black head; white belly; **white outer tail feathers flash when in flight**.
- *slate-colored race*-dark gray above and on breast.
- *Oregon race*-black hood; brown back; pinkish sides.
- *pink-sided race*-pale gray hood; grayish-brown back; broad pink sides and flanks.
- *gray-headed race*-light gray hood and sides; reddish-brown back.

Status: common residents throughout the region and in RMNP.
- slate-colored race is the most widespread in North America; breeds mostly in Canada but winters throughout the region and in RMNP.
- the Oregon junco breeds in conifers in the northern part of the region and winters throughout the region.
- the pink-sided junco breeds in aspen groves as well as conifers in the northern part of the region and winters throughout the region.
- the gray-headed junco breeds above 7,000 feet in the southern half of the region and in RMNP; winters at lower elevations.

These highly adaptable birds inhabit open forests or clearings in dense forests. They frequent open conifer stands with grass understories or aspen-conifer stands with grassy undergrowth. Dark-eyed juncos hop around on the ground picking seeds and insects off the surface. They do not scratch like many of the sparrows.

The females build simple nests of grass on the ground or under a tree, rock or fallen log. Then they lay three to six blue-gray eggs, incubate the eggs and feed the young without help from the males. Raising two broods in a single season is not unusual. Intruders into the nesting territories face agitated adults who flit nearby, uttering a constant barrage of alarm calls.

Very gregarious, dark-eyed juncos usually flock except during the breeding season. As winter approaches, large flocks of these birds move to the lowlands where you can attract them to feeders with offerings of millet or other small seeds.

Dark-eyed Junco (slate-colored)   J. L. Wassink

Dark-eyed Junco (Oregon)   J. L. Wassink

Dark-eyed Junco (gray-headed)   W. Shattil & R. Rozinski

Blackbirds and Orioles (Family Emberizidae, Subfamily Icterinae) are highly visible and vocal birds. They frequently perch on fence posts or on tall reeds or cattails. Their strong, sharply pointed bills enable them to eat a wide variety of food including insects, seeds, grain and berries. Many of the species are dimorphic; the males and females do not look alike. These birds often gather in mixed flocks with other blackbirds and starlings after the breeding season.

Red-winged Blackbird *Agelaius phoeniceus*

Field marks: 9"; *male*-black plumage; sharply pointed bill; **scarlet wing patch with yellow border**; *female*-heavily streaked brown plumage; sharply pointed bill; reddish tint on shoulder.
Status: abundant summer resident throughout the region and in RMNP.

Among the first migrant passerines to return to the region in the spring, the red-winged blackbird's arrival is a sure sign that warmer weather is on the way. The males arrive as early as February and set up territories in the cattails or along wet borders. Several females may nest in the territory of a single male. The females line the nests with fine grasses and suspend the loosely woven cup in a clump of the previous year's cattails. Although they traditionally nested only in marshes, red-winged blackbirds are beginning to colonize grassy fields away from water. Corn, grain, fruit and weed seeds provide nutrition during most of the year except for the breeding season when the young are raised on insects. After raising the young, the adults stay in the marshes while they molt their tail feathers. Some birds stay in the north for the winter but most of them fly south.

Yellow-headed Blackbird *Xanthocephalus xanocephalus*

Field marks: 10"; *male*-black body; **yellow head, neck and chest**; white wing patches visible in flight; *female*-dark grayish-brown plumage; pale yellow throat and upper chest.
Status: common to abundant summer resident throughout the region and in RMNP.

Yellow-headed blackbirds arrive about a month after their red-winged cousins. As with the red-wings, the males arrive first to set up their territories in localized colonies. They pick a conspicuous perch near water from which to sing and display. Their song is harsh and unmusical, something like the creaking of a rusty gate. When the females arrive, they choose a nest site and mate with the male who "owns" that territory. Where yellow-headed blackbirds and red-winged blackbirds share the same marsh, they tend to nest in distinct colonies. Yellow-headed blackbirds usually occupy the cattails and reeds in deeper water while the red-wings nest in the shallower areas.

148

Female Red-winged Blackbird
J. L. Wassink

Male Red-winged Blackbird
J. L. Wassink

Female Yellow-headed Blackbird J. L. Wassink

Male Yellow-headed Blackbird
J. L. Wassink

149

Western Meadowlark — *Sturnella neglecta*

Field marks: 9"; plump profile; streaked brown plumage; long pointed bill; **yellow breast; black neck band; short tail with white outer tail feathers**; tail flicks almost constantly.

Status: common to abundant summer resident in virtually all sagebrush and grassland habitats within the region and in RMNP.

The western meadowlark inhabits open grasslands, cultivated fields and pastures. These common residents build their grass nests on the ground in surprisingly short vegetation, camouflaging the nest by weaving an overhanging dome from nearby grasses. They raise their young on a diet of beetles, crickets, grasshoppers, caterpillars, wasps, ants, spiders and seeds. Watch for meadowlarks perched on a post or wire, singing their exuberant liquid song.

Brewer's Blackbird — *Euphagus cyanocephalus*

Field marks: 9"; *male*-iridescent black plumage; sharply pointed bill; purplish gloss on head; greenish gloss on body; **whitish eye**; *female*-grayish-brown plumage; sharply pointed bill; dark eye.

Status: fairly common to common summer resident throughout the region and in RMNP.

Once strictly a bird of the western United States, the Brewer's blackbird is extending its range across the prairies. A dryland species, it forages on the ground for insects and seeds. As it walks, it jerks its head in a very characteristic manner. The Brewer's blackbird builds a mud and grass nest low in a bush or tree or on the ground, lining the nest with fine plant materials or hair.

Common Grackle — *Quiscalus quiscula*

Field marks: 12"; *male*-glossy black plumage with a blue sheen; long, heavy, pointed bill; **pale yellow eyes; long, wedge-shaped tail**; *female*–dull gray-brown plumage; pale yellow eyes.

Status: common summer resident throughout much of the region and in RMNP.

Grackles inhabit open country near water and city parks. These omnivorous blackbirds feed on insects, seeds and nuts as well as human refuse. The nest is a bulky cup-shaped structure hidden on a horizontal branch of an evergreen. The din that huge groups of these noisy birds create as they communally roost in large stands of trees and the resulting volume of droppings are often unappreciated by nearby residents. The song is merely a rusty squawk.

Western Meadowlark   T. J. Ulrich

Brewer's Blackbird   J. L. Wassink

Common Grackle   J. L. Wassink

Brown-headed Cowbird *Molothrus ater*

Field marks: 7"; *male*-black body; **brown head; short conical bill;** stubby tail; *female*-gray-brown plumage; **short conical bill;** stubby tail.

Status: fairly common summer resident throughout the region and in RMNP.

Brown-headed cowbirds follow grazing cattle or horses to feed on grasshoppers and other insects that the moving animals stir up. Occasionally, a cowbird will perch on the back of one of the animals for a free ride. These birds live along woodland edges, in sagebrush, in creek bottoms and brushy thickets and near agricultural lands. Cowbirds do not build their own nests or raise their own young. Instead, a female will lay single eggs in the nests of as many as 10 or 12 other birds and let the adoptive parents care for them. Yellow warblers, song sparrows, red-winged blackbirds and western wood pewees are just a few of the over 200 species of birds that have served as foster parents to cowbirds. Cowbird eggs hatch in 10 days, usually before those of the host. The young cowbird grows quickly and is usually able to outcompete the rightful nestlings. Although naturally wary, cowbirds can be attracted to ground feeders by regular mixed bird seed.

Northern Oriole *Icterus galbula*

Field marks: 8"; *male*-long pointed bill; **black head,** throat and back; **orange below and on rump;** black wings with white wing bars; *female*-yellowish-gray plumage; dark wings with white wing bars.

Status: fairly common local summer resident throughout the region and in RMNP.

Northern orioles live in the treetops where they search for insects. The semipensile, sac-shaped nest hangs from the tips of the branches of a large tree—often a cottonwood, oak, or other streamside tree. The song is a loud flute-like warble. Two races live in the central Rockies; the "Baltimore" oriole is the more easterly of the two races and the "Bullock's oriole" replaces the "Baltimore" oriole to the west. The "Baltimore oriole" has black cheeks while the similar "Bullock's oriole" has orange cheeks. Attract these birds to feeders with offerings of fruit and sugar water.

Brown-headed Cowbird   J. L. Wassink

Western Wood Pewee nest with Cowbird egg J. L. Wassink

Male Northern Oriole   T. J. Ulrich

153

Finches (Family Fringillidae) are birds whose lives revolve around their food supply. These seed eaters have stout bills with an internal groove to hold the seed in place while the large jaw muscles crush it. The finch uses its tongue to peel and discard the husk. The swallowed kernel passes to the powerful gizzard to be digested. Since finches feed above the snow line, they can and do nest any time of year. They time their nesting to coincide with an abundant supply of seeds. The female builds the cup-shaped nest and incubates the eggs. Both sexes feed the young. While most other birds rely heavily on insects to provide enough protein to their rapidly growing youngsters, several of the finches (crossbills, siskins and redpolls) raise their young on an diet exclusively of seeds. The adults gather large quantities of seeds in their gullet and, at rather infrequent intervals (20-60 minutes), return to the nest to regurgitate seeds to their youngsters. Finches nest solitarily or in loose colonies and defend only a small area immediately around the nest. They often gather in flocks and forage away from the nest wherever they can find an abundance of seeds. When not breeding, they wander erratically in search of food.

Rosy Finch   *Leucosticte arctoa*

Field marks: 6"; reddish belly, flanks and rump.
- *gray-crowned race*-streaked brown plumage; black forehead; gray crown.
- *black race*-black plumage; black forehead; gray crown.
- *brown-capped race*-streaked brown plumage; brown head.

Status: fairly common in the alpine areas of the region;
- the gray-crowned rosy finch breeds in Montana and Canada and may winter anywhere in the region;
- the black rosy finch breeds from central Montana south into Wyoming and may winter anywhere in the region;
- the brown-capped rosy finch breeds in the alpine meadows of Colorado north to central Wyoming and may winter anywhere in the region.

Rosy finches are birds of the mountaintops. They summer on the alpine meadows of the region, constructing a cup-shaped nest in a well-concealed crevice or niche in the rocks. They forage on the ground for seeds and insects, often scouring the margins of melting snowbanks for wind-blown food. During the breeding season, these finches develop cheek-pouches for carrying food—a feature that allows them to conserve energy by carrying large amounts of food on each trip. Rosy finches have long, pointed wings to counteract the strong winds at high elevations.

With the first severe snowstorm of the season, they gather in flocks and seek grassy meadows on the high plateaus and plains of the lower elevations, even venturing as low as the foothills and plains in some years. There they roost in rock crevices and feed on the ground on weed and grass seed.

Rosy Finch (gray-crowned)   J. L. Wassink

Rosy Finch (black)   VIREO, H. Cruickshank

Rosy Finch (brown-capped)   K. Dannen & D. Dannen

155

Pine Grosbeak
Pinicola enucleator

Field marks: 9"; *male*-**reddish-pink plumage; short heavy bill**; white wing bars; *female*-olive-gray plumage; short heavy bill.

Status: fairly common permanent resident throughout the coniferous forests of the region and in RMNP.

The largest of the finches, pine grosbeaks have rounded bills ideally suited to their diet of needle buds and berries. They are also capable of extracting and crushing pine seeds. These plump, slow-moving birds of the subalpine coniferous forests build their nests in the low branches of an alpine fir or an Engelmann spruce. As winter approaches, pine grosbeaks move to lower elevations to feed on pinyon nuts or the fruit of ornamental trees. Their song is a musical warble.

Red Crossbill
Loxia curvirostra

Field marks: 6"; *male*-brick red plumage; **crossed mandibles**; black, unbarred wings; *female*-olive-gray plumage; crossed mandibles; unbarred wings.

Status: local resident and irregular vagrant in the region and in RMNP.

Red crossbills live in coniferous forests where the cone crop is abundant. The birds dangle upside down to extract seeds or snip off cones. They carry the cones to a perch and hold them down with one foot while they extract the seeds. The crossed tips of the bill aid in prying open the tough pine, spruce and fir cones. Once the birds open the cones, they use their tongues to scoop out the seeds. Their bold and deliberate manner allows birders to observe them quite closely.

Red crossbills are unique in that they may nest almost any time of year when sufficient conifer seeds are available—even when the days are short and snow is on the ground. Where pine seeds are available, they nest in the spring. In larch forests, they will nest in late summer. Where they depend on spruce seeds, crossbills nest in fall and early winter. In mixed spruce and pine forests, nesting may stretch over ten months of the year. In Colorado, crossbill nests with young have been found in every month except October and November. In Wyoming, they nest in all months from February through August. When not breeding, red crossbills wander erratically, searching for abundant supplies of cones.

Female Pine Grosbeak
T. J. Ulrich

Male Pine Grosbeak
T. J. Ulrich

Female Red Crossbill
J. L. Wassink

Male Red Crossbill
J. L. Wassink

157

Cassin's Finch   *Carpodacus cassinii*

Field marks: 6"; *male*-heavily streaked plumage; **reddish wash on head and throat; light, unstreaked belly;** *female*-heavily streaked plumage.

Status: fairly common residents throughout the region and in RMNP.

Cassin's finches make their homes in higher elevation coniferous forests. They prefer open, rather dry forests or forest edges. Their short stout bills are ideal for cracking seeds, which they eat along with insects, buds and small fruits. During the spring breeding season, male Cassin's finches sing a varied, liquid, warbling song. They build their nests from 15 to 60 feet above the ground in a conifer. The well-constructed nests of dry plant materials, rootlets, hair and sometimes decorated with lichens cradle four or five eggs. The male feeds the female on the nest while she incubates but he does not share in the nest-sitting duties. Distinguishing the Cassin's finch from the purple finch is difficult because individual variations in shade, intensity and distribution of color may overlap from one species to the other. Differentiating the birds' songs and calls allows for positive identification—but you will need to listen to recordings to learn to do this.

House Finch   *Carpodacus mexicanus*

Field marks: 5"; *male*-**short stubby bill;** streaked brown plumage; red forehead, eyebrow and throat; **streaked sides;** *female*-strongly streaked brown plumage.

Status: uncommon to common throughout the region and in RMNP; abundant in urban areas.

House finches occupy the lowlands of the region, often living in arid scrub, chaparral, open woodlands and urban areas. They have adapted well to humans. House finches traditionally nested in cavities in cactuses and mesquite but have extended their range to nest in the abundant nooks and crannies in buildings. Unlike most songbirds, they do not carry out the fecal sacs of the young and so the nests get rather messy. These finches feed primarily on seeds but also eat buds, flowers and some insects. Attract them to feeders with sunflower seeds. They sing a loud melodious song. Males in some areas have a yellow wash instead of the usual red coloration, possibly a result of nutritional differences.

Male Cassin's Finch   J. L. Wassink

Female Cassin's Finch   J. L. Wassink

House Finch   T. J. Ulrich

159

Common Redpoll
Carduelis flammea

Field marks: 5"; brown and gray streaked plumage; **red cap; black chin;** pink breast; heavily streaked flanks.

Status: irregular winter visitor throughout the region and in RMNP.

Common redpolls breed in the subarctic forests of northern Canada. In winter, they wander erratically in search of food—weed seeds, birch cones and well-supplied bird feeders. Only occasionally wandering into southern Colorado, they frequent the open habitats of desert shrub, sagebrush, grasslands and urban areas.

Pine Siskin
Carduelis pinus

Field marks: 5"; small size; thin pointed bill; **heavily streaked brown above;** streaked white below; **yellow often visible in wings and at base of tail** .

Status: common residents in the coniferous forests of the region and in RMNP.

Noisy, gregarious and nomadic, pine siskins fly in groups, uttering light twittering notes that seem to be synchronized with their wingbeats. These treetop birds often hang upside down as they use their tweezer-like bills to extract the seeds of small cones or to feed on tree buds and small leaves. They are seek out dandelion seeds when those are available. They raise their broods in well-constructed, compact nests of dry roots, grasses and leaves set well up in a conifer. Their tame dispositions make them a joy at feeders where they come readily to thistle (niger) seeds. Their call is a rising, high-pitched buzzy trill. Like many of the other finches, they wander erratically in winter.

American Goldfinch
Carduelis tristis

Field marks: 5"; *male*-**bright black and yellow color pattern**; black forehead; **black wings** with white wing bars; *female*-greenish-yellow color; **black wings** with white wing bars.

Status: fairly common seasonal resident throughout the region, rare in RMNP.

American goldfinches depend heavily on thistles. They line their nests with thistle down and raise their young on a diet of thistle seeds, and therefore time their nesting to coincide with the maturing of thistle seeds. Consequently, they are the last birds in the region to nest. Their tweezer-like bills are ideal for extracting seeds from thistles and other composites. In fact, the American goldfinch is the only bird capable of eating teasel seeds, which are located at the base of long, spiked tubes. After the nesting season, goldfinches gather in flocks to forage in open weedy fields and thickets. They winter in river bottoms of the region. Their call is a "per-chic-er-re." Attract them to feeders with thistle seeds.

Common Redpoll   T. J. Ulrich

Pine Siskin   J. L. Wassink

Male American Goldfinch   J. L. Wassink

161

Evening Grosbeak   *Coccothraustes vespertinus*

Field marks: 8"; big, clumsy-looking birds; black and yellow color pattern; heavy powerful bill; heavy yellow eyebrow; **black wings with large white wing patches**; *female*-duller colors than the male.

Status: fairly common local resident throughout the region and in RMNP.

Evening grosbeaks are birds of the coniferous forests. In the fall, following the breeding season, they gather into sometimes large flocks and make sporadic appearances at sources of abundant food supplies such as areas with heavy cone crops or well-stocked bird feeders. Their bills are adapted to cracking hard seeds and extracting seeds from conifer cones. Evening grosbeaks love sunflower seeds and flocks of them may spend most of the winter at a single feeder. They also love the seeds of boxelders, willows, maples and elms as well as ripening chokecherries.

Weaver Finches (Family Passeridae) are primarily an Old World
family of birds. Named for the nest-weaving habits of some of its members—who weave the largest and most complex nests in the bird world—weaver finches have short, conical bills adapted to cracking seeds. Two introduced species represent this family in North America: the European tree sparrow and the house sparrow. Only the house sparrow lives in the central Rockies.

House Sparrow   *Passer domesticus*

Field marks: 6"; *male*-brown and gray plumage; black bill; gray crown; **black throat and upper breast**; white cheeks; **chestnut nape**; white wing bars; *female*-gray-brown plumage; pale eyebrow; gray below.

Status: abundant resident throughout the region around developed areas; absent in remote habitats.

This introduced species has flourished in the United States. Bold and impudent and yet suspicious and wary, house sparrows were brought from Great Britain and introduced into Brooklyn, New York, in the 1850s. They have since taken up residence wherever human construction has provided small cracks or crevices for nesting. Into those openings, house sparrows pack grass, paper and feathers to form a rather messy nest. Where crevices are not available, they build round, dome-shaped nests in trees or shrubs. These noisy and gregarious birds feed on seeds and whatever scraps of food they can find. Aggressive when competing for nesting sites and food, they displace many native species and, so, raise the ire of birders everywhere.

Male Evening Grosbeak   J. L. Wassink

Female Evening Grosbeak   J. L. Wassink

Male House Sparrow   J. L. Wassink

Suggested References

Bird Identification

Farrand, John Jr. *The Audubon Society Master Guide to Birding.* Alfred A Knopf, New York, 1983, 3 volumes.

Harrison, Hal H. *A Field Guide to Western Birds' Nests.* Houghton Mifflin Company, Boston, 1979, 279 pp.

Kaufman, Kenn. *Advanced Birding.* Houghton Mifflin Company, Boston, 1990, 299 pp.

Robbins, Chandler S., Bertel Bruun, and Herbert S. Zim. *Birds of North America.* Golden Press, Racine, Wisconsin, 1983, 360 pp.

Udvardy, Miklos D. F. *The Audubon Society Field Guide to North American Birds - Western Region.* Alfred A. Knopf, New York, 1977, 855 pp.

Bird Behavior

Dennis, John V. *Beyond the Bird Feeder.* Alfred A. Knopf, New York, 1981, 201 pp.

Stokes, Donald W. and Lillian Q. Stokes. *A Guide to Bird Behavior.* Little, Brown and Company, Boston, 1983, 3 volumes.

Locating and Observing Birds

Brainerd, John W. *The Nature Observer's Handbook.* The Glove Pequot Press, Chester, Connecticut, 1986, 255 pp.

Chase, Charles A., et al. *Colorado Bird Distribution Latilong Study.* The Colorado Field Ornithologists, 1982, 82 pp.

Hanenkrat, Frank T. *Wildlife Watcher's Handbook.* Winchester Press, New York, 1977, 241 pp.

Heintzelman, Donald S. *A Manual for Bird Watching in the Americas.* Universe Books, New York, 1979, 255 pp.

Jones, Jown Oliver. *Where the Birds Are.* William Morrow and Company Inc., New York, 1990, 400 pp.

Kress, Stephen W. *The Audubon Society Handbook for Birders.* Charles Scribner's Sons, New York, 1981, 322 pp.

McElroy, Thomas P. *The Habitat Guide to Birding.* Alfred A. Knopf, New York, 1974, 268 pp.

Pettingill, Olin Sewall. *A Guide to Bird Finding West of the Mississippi.* Oxford University Press, New York, 1981, 781 pp.

Riley, Laura and William. *Guide to the National Wildlife Refuges.* Anchor Press/Doubleday, Garden City, New York, 1979, 653 pp.

Attracting Birds

Kress, Stephen W. *The Audubon Society Guide to Attracting Birds.* Charles Scribner's Sons, New York, 377 pp.

Mahnken, Jan. *Feeding the Birds.* Garden Way Publishing, Pownal, Vermont, 1983, 186 pp.

Mahnken, Jan. *Hosting the Birds.* Garden Way Publishing, Pownal, Vermont, 1989, 208 pp.

Bird Songs

Audible Audubon. National Audubon Society, 1977.

Borror, Donald J. *Songs of Western Birds.* Dover Publications, New York, 1971, 12" 33⅓ rpm, record album.

A Field Guide to Western Bird Songs. Laboratory of Ornithology, Cornell University, New York, 1975, 3 C-60 cassettes.

Periodicals and Organizations

American Birds
Published 6 times a year by the National Audubon Society. Contact: *American Birds,* 950 Third Avenue, New York, NY 10022.

Birding
Published 6 times a year by the American Birding Association, Inc. Contact: American Birding Association, Inc., P. O. Box 6599, Colorado Springs, CO 80934.

The Living Bird Quarterly
Published 4 times a year by the Cornell University Laboratory of Ornithology. Contact: Cornell University Laboratory of Ornithology, 159 Sapsucker Woods Road, Ithaca, NY 14850.

Bird Watcher's Digest
Published 6 times a year. Contact: *Bird Watcher's Digest*, P.O. Box 110, Marietta, OH 45750.

Birder's World
Published 6 times a year. Contact *Birder's World*, Inc., 720 E. 8th Street, Holland, MI 49423.

WildBird
Published monthly. Contact: *Wildbird* Magazine, P.O. Box 483, Mt. Morris, IL 61054-0483.

Glossary

abundant species - a species that you are likely to see 25 or more of per day when you look in the appropriate habitat during the appropriate season.

alpine - inhabiting or growing in the mountains above timberline.

altricial - young that hatch blind, naked and helpless.

brackish - mixture of fresh and salt water.

breeder - a bird that nests and raises young within the area.

brood - young birds that hatch from a single clutch of eggs.

cambium - the layer of soft, growing tissue between the bark and wood of trees and shrubs.

carrion - dead and decaying flesh.

clutch - a group of eggs laid by one bird.

comb - a thick fleshy growth on the top of the head.

common species - a species that you will see daily when looking in the right habitat during the right season.

coniferous - cone-bearing plants.

crest - a tuft of elongated feathers extending backward on top of the head.

crown - the top of the head.

deciduous - plants that drop their leaves every year.

dimorphic -usually refers to species in which the sexes differ in color but may refer to species that have two different color phases.

diurnal - active during the daylight hours.

emergents - aquatic plants that are rooted underwater but grow up out of the water, such as reeds and cattails.

estuary - the mouth of a river where the fresh water meets the sea and water levels are influenced by the tides.

fairly common species - a species that you will likely see once every three days when looking in the right habitat during the right season.

fledge - the act of leaving the nest; usually occurs after the young are fully feathered and able to fly.

foliage - leaves of a tree or bush.

gizzard - a heavily muscled organ that aids digestion of hard seeds by mechanically grinding them down.

gorget - brilliant feathers covering the throats of male hummingbirds.

gregarious - birds that habitually associate with others in flocks.

gular - of, relating to or situated on the throat.

hawking - pursuing or attacking prey while flying.

horns - tufts of feathers that extend upward from the sides of the head.

incubate - keep eggs warm until they hatch.

iridescent - shiny, almost metallic feather color that results from the diffraction of light rays and not from pigmentation—such as the gorgets of male hummingbirds.

irregular species - a species that is abundant in the region at times but extremely rare most of the time.

larvae - immature young of insects and invertebrates.

lek - a traditional site where male birds of certain species, such as sharp-tailed grouse, gather to perform courtship displays to attract females.

monogamous - a species that breeds with only one individual during a breeding cycle.

montane - pertaining to, growing in or inhabiting mountainous regions, the lower vegetation belt on the mountains.

molt - the process of shedding and replacing feathers that usually occurs after the breeding season and before the fall migration.

mustache - a strip of colored feathers extending backward from the base of the bill.

nape - the back of the head, just above the neck.

nictitating membrane - a clear secondary eyelid that cleans the eye and protects it during swift flight, underwater swimming, when flying through thick brush, etc.

nocturnal - active during the night.

nomadic - wandering from place to place, seemingly without a pattern.

omnivorous - an organism that eats both vegetable and animal matter.

plumage - the feathers of a bird.

polygamous - a species that breeds with more than one mate during a single breeding cycle.

precocious - well developed, covered with down and able to leave the nest and run about soon after hatching.

prehensile - capable of precise movement and adapted for grasping or holding by wrapping around.

primaries - the outermost and longest flight feathers of the wing.

prolific - able to produce large numbers of offspring.

raptors - a bird of prey such as a hawk or eagle.

rare species - a species that appears in the region only a few times each year.

resident species - a species that lives in the region year-round.

rump - the back portion of a bird just above the base of the tail feathers.

scapulars - the group of feathers on the shoulder of the bird, along side the back.

scavenger - a bird that feeds on carrion, garbage or the leftovers of other birds' kills.

solitary - a bird that prefers to live alone and avoids the company of others of its species.

spatulate - spoon shaped.

species - a group of animals or plants exhibiting common characteristics that interbreed and produce fertile young when given the opportunity.

stoop - a swift dive in pursuit of prey, characteristic of many raptors.

summer resident - a species that lives in the region only during the spring and summer.

territory - a section of habitat that an individual or breeding pair actively defend against others of its species.

thermals - rising currents of air resulting from the unequal heating of the earth's surface; often used by soaring birds to gain altitude or remain aloft with minimal effort.

torpor - a state in which the metabolism drops to abnormally low levels; a means of conserving energy.

uncommon species - a species that you will see no more than once in a week of looking.

vagrant - a bird that does not normally visit the region but may occasionally wander through.

wing-coverts - small feathers that overlap and cover the bases of the large flight feathers.

winter visitor - a species that frequents the region between mid-December and late February.

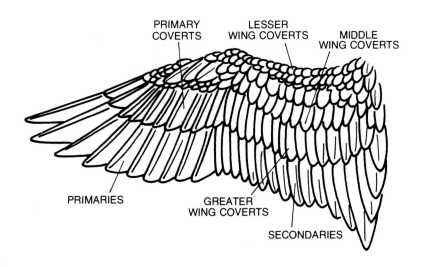

DUCK WING
Upper Surface

Mike Ulrich

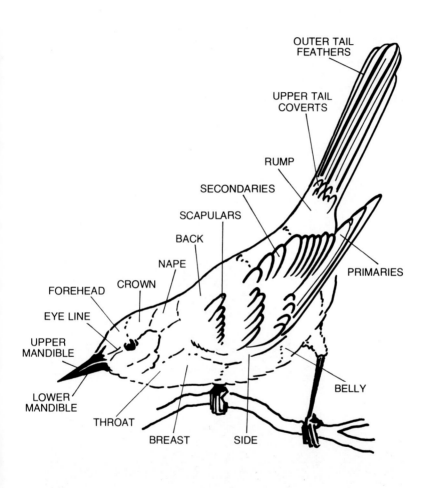

OUTER TAIL
FEATHERS

UPPER TAIL
COVERTS

RUMP

SECONDARIES

SCAPULARS

BACK

NAPE

PRIMARIES

FOREHEAD   CROWN

EYE LINE

UPPER
MANDIBLE

BELLY

LOWER
MANDIBLE

THROAT

BREAST   SIDE

Mike Ulrich

PARTS OF A BIRD

Peregrine Falcon

J. L. Wassink

Index

We encourage you to patronize your local bookstores. Most stores will order any title that they do not stock. You may also order directly from Mountain Press by mail, using the order form provided below or by calling our toll-free number and using your Visa or MasterCard. We will gladly send you a complete catalog upon request.

Some other Natural History titles of interest:

____A Guide to Rock Art Sites Southern California and Southern Nevada	$20.00
____Alpine Wildflowers of the Rocky Mountains	$14.00
____Beachcombing the Atlantic Coast	$15.00
____Birds of the Central Rockies	$14.00
____Birds of the Northern Rockies	$12.00
____Birds of the Pacific Northwest Mountains	$14.00
____Coastal Wildflowers of the Pacific Northwest	$14.00
____Edible and Medicinal Plants of the West	$21.00
____Graced by Pines The Ponderosa Pine in the American West	$10.00
____Hollows, Peepers, and Highlands An Appalachian Mountain Ecology	$14.00
____An Introduction to Northern California Birds	$14.00
____An Introduction to Southern California Birds	$14.00
____The Lochsa Story Land Ethics in the Bitterroot Mountains	$20.00
____Mammals of the Central Rockies	$14.00
____Mammals of the Northern Rockies	$12.00
____Mountain Plants of the Pacific Northwest	$20.00
____New England's Mountain Flowers	$17.00
____Northwest Weeds The Ugly and Beautiful Villains of Fields, Gardens, and Roadsides	$14.00
____Owls, Whoo are they?	$12.00
____Plants of Waterton-Glacier National Parks and the Northern Rockies	$12.00
____Roadside Plants of Southern California	$14.00
____Sagebrush Country A Wildflower Sanctuary	$14.00
____Watchable Birds of the Northern Rockies	$14.00
____Watchable Birds of the Southwest	$14.00

Please include $3.00 per order to cover shipping and handling.

Send the books marked above. I enclose $_____

Name_____

Address_____

City_____State_____Zip_____

l Payment enclosed (check or money order in U.S. funds)
Bill my: l VISA   l MasterCard   Expiration Date:_____

Card No._____

Signature_____

Mountain Press Publishing Company
P.O. Box 2399 • Missoula, MT 59806
Order Toll Free 1-800-234-5308
Have your Visa or MasterCard ready.